sewing

HOME
for the

Over 50 stylish projects to give your home a fresh look

CREATIVE
PUBLISHING
international

CHANHASSEN, MINNESOTA
www.creativepub.com

Copyright © 2002
Creative Publishing international, Inc.
18705 Lake Drive East
Chanhassen, Minnesota 55317
1-800-328-3895
www.creativepub.com
All rights reserved
Printed in U.S.A.

President/CEO: Michael Eleftheriou
Vice President/Publisher: Linda Ball
Vice President/Retail Sales: Kevin Haas

SEWING FOR THE HOME
Created by: The Editors of Creative Publishing
 international, Inc.

Executive Editor: Alison Brown Cerier
Senior Editor: Linda Neubauer
Project Managers: Linnéa Christensen, Kathi Holmes
Senior Art Director: Stephanie Michaud
Cover Designer: Megan Noller
Desktop Publishing Specialist: Laurie Kristensen
Editorial Intern: Andrew Karre
Project & Prop Stylist: Joanne Wawra
Sewing Staff: Karen Cermak, Arlene Dohrman, Sharon
 Ecklund, Phyllis Galbraith, Valerie Hill, Kristi Kuhnau,
 Virginia Mateen, Ginger Mountin, Carol Pilot,
 Michelle Skudlarek, Nancy Sundeen
Technical Photo Stylists: Jennifer Bailey, Karen Cermak,
 Arlene Dohrman, Bridget Haugh, Susan Jorgensen
Studio Services Manager: Marcia Chambers
Photo Services Coordinator: Carol Osterhus
Lead Photographer: Charles Nields
Photographers: Rebecca Hawthorne, Kevin Hedden,
 Rex Irmen, Billy Lindner, Mark Macemon, Mike Parker,
 Andrea Rugg, Greg Wallace
Director of Production Services: Kim Gerber
Shop Manager: Daniel Widerski
Contributors: American and Efird, Inc./Mettler; Conso
 Products Company; Dritz Corporation; General Clutch;
 Graber Industries, Inc./Springs Window Fashion Division;
 Handler Textile Corporation; Kirsch Division, Cooper
 Industries, Inc.; Krifon; Joyce Oakle; The Singer Company;
 Springs Industries; Swavelle/Mill Creek Textiles; Waverly,
 Division of F. Schumacher & Company

ISBN 1-58923-076-0

Printed on American paper by:
R. R. Donnelley
10 9 8 7 6 5 4 3

Creative Publishing international, Inc. offers a variety of
how-to books. For information write:
    Creative Publishing international, Inc.
     Subscriber Books
    18705 Lake Drive East
    Chanhassen, MN 55317

sewing
HOME
for the

Over 50 stylish projects to give your home a fresh look

CONTENTS

How to Use This Book 7

Fabrics for Home Decorating 9

Equipment & Notions 12

Machine Stitching 16

Hand Stitching 20

Padded Work Surface 21

Windows

Window Fashions 24

Curtains 29

Rod Pockets & Headings . . .30

Lining Rod-pocket Curtains . .33

Ruffled Curtains 34

Tab-top Curtains 38

Tiebacks 40

Easy Pleated Draperies 44

Shades 47

Roman Shade 48

Stitched-tuck Shade 52

Hobbled Shade 53

Cloud Shade 54

Balloon Shade 56

Insulated Roman Shade 59

Roller Shade 63

Pillows

Pillow Fashions 68

Knife-edge Pillow or Liner . . .70

Welted Knife-edge Pillow . . .72

Mock Box Pillow 74

Mock Welted Pillow 76

Box Pillow 77

Ruffled Pillow 78

Flange Pillows 80

Shirred Pillows 82

Neckroll Pillows 84

Pillow Closures 86

Cushions 89

Tufted Cushion 91

Cushion Ties 92

Hook & Loop Tabs 93

Tables

Tabletop Fashions 96

Round Tablecloths 98

Square & Rectangular
    Tablecloths 100

Quilted Table Covers 101

Placemats, Table Runners
    & Table Mats 102

Banded Placemats 104

Trimmed Placemats 105

Napkins 107

Bed & Bath

Bed Fashions 110

Comforter 113

Comforter Cover 114

Pillow Shams 116

Dust Ruffles & Bed Skirts . .119

Shower Curtain 122

Index 124

How to Use This Book

Sewing for the Home has a wide selection of decorator home fashions for you to sew. In making these items, we have considered cost, simplicity of construction, ease of care, and coordination of colors and patterns. We have also considered the amount of time involved; many of these projects can be completed in an afternoon or evening. Also included are designer customizing hints which you can incorporate into your home decorating projects.

Home Sewing Basics

We start with the basics of fabric and color selection, then show you how to use your sewing machine and its standard equipment to achieve the best sewing results. You will also learn about optional machine attachments that make home decorator sewing faster and easier.

Instructions for many of the projects include alternate sewing methods and suggest timesaving techniques such as fusible web to join two fabrics, fusible backing to stabilize a tieback, or self-styling tapes for pleating or gathering.

Before you begin to sew, read the information on pages 9 through 21 to acquaint yourself with the basic techniques of home decorator sewing.

Step-by-Step Guidance

This book is divided into four project sections: windows, pillows, tables, and bed and bath. For windows, we give instructions for favorite treatments like pinch-pleated draperies and rod-pocket curtains, along with directions for many other window fashions, including five Roman shade variations. Pillows range from simple knife-edge styles to pillows with flanged or shirred edges. For tables, learn to make round and rectangular tablecloths, quilted runners, bordered placemats, and six different styles of napkins. Make a

comforter for your bed or cover an old one, then sew pillow shams and a dust ruffle to match. Coordinate your bath with a custom shower curtain.

At the beginning of each section is an overview of the section. This includes how to take accurate measurements for the projects and what to consider when selecting fabric and sewing aids. Cutting directions are detailed at the beginning of each project. For easy reference, fabrics and notions required to complete the project are included in boxes labeled YOU WILL NEED.

The step-by-step instructions that are given are complete; you do not need to purchase additional patterns. The photographs that accompany the instructions show you how the project should look at each step of its construction.

The sewing techniques you learn for one project can be applied to others. The same method is used for making ruffles on curtains as for pillows or bed accessories. The technique for mitering corners on a tablecloth is the same as on pillows or placemats.

Easy Home Decorator Projects

Experienced sewers can manage any of the projects we have designed; other projects such as knife-edge pillows, shower curtains, napkins, or roller shades are suitable for less experienced sewers.

The projects throughout this book can be made with coordinating fabrics. One fabric can be used for many different projects. Start with one project as the focal point of the room, then turn leftover fabrics from larger projects into attractive, coordinating accessories.

We hope the step-by-step guidance, practical shortcuts, and designer tips given in *Sewing for the Home* encourage you to design and create your own home decorator fashions.

Fabrics for Home Decorating

Knowledge of fibers, finishes, and fabrics will help you select the best fabrics for home sewing. Fiber and finish information is on the bolt-end label or printed on the selvage of decorator fabrics.

Terms to Know

Fiber is the basic unit of yarn before it is made into fabric. Fiber content affects durability and care.

Natural fibers come from nature. They include wool, cotton, silk, and linen (flax). Natural fibers are durable, natural insulators.

Man-made fibers are chemically produced. Man-made fibers such as polyester, nylon, and acrylic are usually associated with easy-care features and are well suited to home sewing projects.

Blends are combinations of fibers utilizing the best qualities of two or more fibers in one fabric.

A finish is a treatment to a fabric to change its behavior or improve its appearance, care, or *hand* (how it feels). Finishes can make a fabric crease-resistant, mildew-resistant, resistant to oil or water-borne stains, or add luster and stability.

A permanent finish is often used to describe crease-resistance and shrinkage-resistance. Few finishes are truly permanent for the life of the fabric. Although they are durable, they may become less effective with laundering and drycleaning.

Decorator fabrics are designed for home decorator projects. They are usually 48" or 54" (122 or 137 cm) wide and often have special finishes which are desirable for home items.

Fashion fabrics are used primarily for dressmaker or fashion sewing; however, fabrics such as calico, eyelet, poplin, polished cotton, gingham, sateen, and muslin may also be used for the home.

Repeat is the size (length and width) of the pattern or motif printed on the fabric. You will usually need to buy one extra repeat for each length of fabric you use. The size of the repeat is often printed on the label or marked on the selvage of decorator fabric.

Selvage is the finished lengthwise edge of a woven fabric.

Grain is the direction in which fabric yarns run. Woven fabrics consist of lengthwise yarns intersecting crosswise yarns. When these yarns cross each other at perfect right angles the fabric is *on-grain*. If the intersection of lengthwise and crosswise yarns is not at right angles the fabric is *off-grain*. Avoid buying fabric that is printed off-grain; it is difficult to work with and will not hang properly.

Other Practical Considerations

Washable fabrics should be prewashed. Other fabrics should be preshrunk by steaming with an iron. Many fabrics are treated with finishes to protect their beauty and resist soiling. Washing may remove this finish, alter the fabric's hand, or fade the colors. Dryclean your finished projects to keep them looking their best. If you do wash, use cold water and nondetergent soap.

Fabric Selection Guide

Project	Fabric Suggestions	Appropriate Finishes
Curtains, draperies	Lightweight sheer and semi-sheer fabrics: cotton, cotton-polyester blends, organdy, dotted Swiss, lace, batiste, voile. Mediumweight opaque fabrics such as textured and nubby cotton, linen and blends; open weaves; smooth surfaces such as chintz, polished cotton, antique satin, silk, moire.	Oil and water repellent; sunfast; mildew resistant; preshrunk so that residual shrinkage will not exceed 1% in either direction.
Shades	For Roman shades and roller shades: closely woven fabrics such as sailcloth, denim, poplin, polished cotton. For cloud and balloon shades: semi-sheers and lightweight fabrics such as dotted Swiss, eyelet, cotton-polyester blends.	Oil and water repellent; sunfast; mildew resistant; preshrunk so that residual shrinkage will not exceed 1% in either direction.
Linings, pillow liners	White or off-white sateen, muslin, sheeting.	Preshrunk linings for washable curtains and draperies.
Pillows, cushions	Closely woven fabrics to retain their shape, such as polished or textured cottons and linens, chintz, velveteen, corduroy.	Oil and water repellent, soil and stain-release.
Tablecloths, napkins, placemats	Polished or textured cotton, linen, calico, cotton-polyester blends, quilted fabrics, loosely woven homespun-type cottons.	Oil and water repellent, soil and stain-release.
Comforters, covers, shams, dust ruffles	Closely woven, washable fabrics: sheets, brushed cotton flannel, polished cotton, chintz. For ruffles: eyelet, dotted Swiss, lace.	Washable, colorfast; easy-care.

Mixing & Matching Fabrics

Using a number of complementary patterns and colors helps to connect areas in rooms and give your home continuity.

Geometric prints, stripes, patterns, and solids can work together to give a room style and interest. Fabric manufacturers make it easy to coordinate fabrics by designing groups of complementary patterns, prints, and solids which you can use in any combination.

If you coordinate fabrics on your own, unroll the bolts and compare them side-by-side in natural light. Examine the fabrics from several angles to judge the compatibility of print and color.

Bolts often come from different dye lots. To avoid problems of slight color variations or differences in pattern printing, buy fabrics for large projects from only one bolt. Check patterned fabrics to be sure they are printed on the straight grain. Also remember that wider fabrics generally mean fewer seams, especially in curtains.

Consider where the fabric will be used and how it relates to other fabrics in the room. Most stores have display cuts or swatch books of their decorator fabrics available. They may permit you to take swatches home. This gives you a chance to see the fabric next to other fabrics and lets you see it in your home lighting, which may be very different from store lighting. If swatches are not available, ask for a sample from the bolt or buy a small piece before you invest in a large cut.

Choosing Colors

Keep these points in mind as you shop for fabrics.

• What colors already exist in the room? Take paint chips, carpet swatches, or small cushions with you when you compare fabric.

• What wood tones are in your room? Fabric colors can enhance the natural tones and richness of wood.

• Color affects your mood. Pastels, neutrals, and cooler shades, such as blues and some greens, are soothing. Bright shades and warmer colors like reds and yellows tend to stimulate. Dark colors create a cozy feeling.

• Color alters perceptions. Colors appear darker against light backgrounds, lighter against dark surfaces. Warm colors make objects seem larger, while cool colors make them recede. In general, avoid using bold, contrasting colors in small rooms.

• Keep the room's exposure in mind. You may want to warm a northern exposure with warm tones, or cool down a hot sunny room with pale blues.

• Light colors show soil more readily than dark colors.

• At windows, pale colors diffuse light while dark colors block it. Hold up a length of fabric in direct sunlight to see if it creates the effect you want.

• Finally, consider your own preferences. Use these guidelines and your own taste to choose colors and patterns that beautify your home and reflect your personal style.

Equipment & Notions

The Basics

Home decorator sewing requires the same basic equipment as dressmaker sewing, with the addition of tools for measuring windows and furniture. Using the proper equipment makes the work easier and the results more satisfying.

1) **Needle threader** eases threading of hand and machine needles.

2) **Pins** with plastic or glass heads are easier to see and handle.

3) **Thimble** protects your middle finger when you sew by hand.

4) **Needles** for general hand sewing are *sharps*. Buy a package of assorted sizes for various sewing tasks.

5) **T-pins** are long, sturdy, broad-headed pins often used in professional drapery workrooms.

6) **Quilting pins** are extra long and useful for working with heavy or thick materials.

7) **All-purpose thread** is used for hand and machine sewing on most fabrics. Choose cotton-wrapped polyester or all-polyester thread for durability.

Measuring Tools

The most important consideration in home decorator sewing is accurate measuring. The following measuring aids help you make correct calculations for buying and cutting fabric.

1) **Carpenter's square** is an L-shaped ruler, used to determine the perfect right angles and square corners that are essential to the fit of curtains, shades, tablecloths, and pillows.

2) **Wood folding ruler** is used for measuring large areas. Because of its stability, this ruler is more accurate than a tape measure.

3) **Yardstick** is used for measuring long, flat lengths of fabric, and for marking and squaring grain lines. The surface of the yardstick should be smooth so it does not snag fabric.

4) **Spring-return metal tape** measures windows and other large areas. It is also handy for measuring around curves.

5) **Seam gauge** makes quick, short measurements such as those for hems. The 6" (15 cm) metal or plastic ruler has a sliding marker for accuracy in measuring.

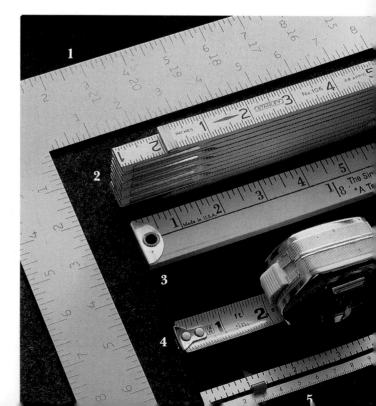

Marking & Cutting Tools

After making careful calculations and taking accurate measurements, mark and cut the fabric in preparation for sewing. Have on hand an assortment of marking tools for various fabric colors and textures. Good quality cutting tools are also a smart investment.

1) Cutting board is marked with horizontal and vertical lines, and is useful for laying out and cutting lengths of fabric up to 2 yards (1.85 meters). It is made of heavy cardboard so fabric can be pinned in place. Two board lengths may be necessary for large items such as floor-length curtains.

2) Tailor's chalk is specially designed to mark directly on fabric and rub off easily.

3) Trimmers have straight handles and are used for trimming and straightening edges. A lightweight, slim blade aids accuracy.

4) Seam ripper is used to remove stitches. Use it with care to avoid ripping fabric.

5) Bent-handled shears allow fabric to remain flat during cutting. Shears should be lightweight, easy to handle, and 8" or 9" (20.5 or 23 cm) long.

6) Liquid marking pens make sharp, defined lines on firm fabrics. One type of pen makes a mark that can be removed with clear water; the other makes a mark that disappears within 48 hours. Test marking pens on a fabric scrap before using. Ironing permanently sets the markings; if markings are on the right side of the fabric, do not press until they are removed.

Notions

Notions serve three purposes in home decor sewing. Some, such as the rings used on Roman shades, are essential to the construction of an item; others, such as fusible web and fray preventer, make sewing easier. Notions such as flat braids, welting, and ribbons are simply decorative.

1) Decorative trims such as welting, flat braids, and ribbons are available in a wide range of colors and styles to complement the items you sew. Select trims with the same care requirements as the fabric.

2) Cording in various diameters is available for covering with your fabric to make welting.

3) Fusible web, with or without paper backing, is used for hemming or for bonding two layers of fabric together. It is available in narrow strips for hems, or in 18" (46 cm) widths for fusing larger areas.

4) Fabric adhesives such as glue stick and craft or white glue may be used for temporary basting or for permanently applying batting or trims to items which will not receive much handling.

5) Liquid fray preventer dries invisibly and prevents the raw edge of fabric from fraying. Use it as a temporary agent to prevent raveling while working with fabric or as a permanent finish on exposed seams and edges.

6) Plastic rings in assorted sizes are useful for making Roman shades or for attaching tiebacks.

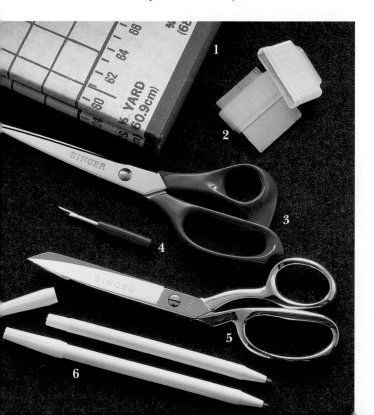

Timesaving Notions & Equipment

Home decorating projects often involve large expanses of fabric with long seams and hems. An assortment of convenient notions and equipment is available to simplify these tasks. Some items are accessories for the sewing machine that are available from your machine dealer. Be sure to purchase a style that fits your machine. Other items can be found in the notions department of the fabric store.

Rotary cutter and mat are indispensible in the sewing room for quick, accurate cutting. The cutters are available in two sizes: the smaller size works well for cutting curves, lightweight fabrics, or a few layers of fabric; the larger size works well for cutting heavier fabrics or multiple layers in long, straight edges. For easy measuring and cutting, the rotary cutter is guided alongside a wide, clear plastic ruler. The cutting mat protects the blade and the table. A mat printed with a grid is helpful for measuring and for cutting right angles. Mats come in a variety of sizes; the larger the better for cutting home decorating projects.

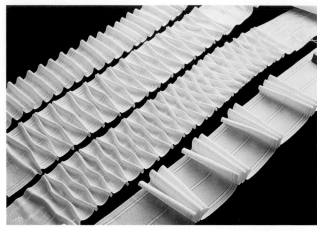

Self-styling tapes make quick work of gathering or pleating the upper edge of curtains or cloud shades. They are available in various widths and styles, as either fusible or sew-in tapes. Cords woven into the tape are pulled to create the characteristic pattern of pleats or gathers.

Walking foot feeds top and bottom layers of fabric at the same rate, ensuring that seams start and end evenly. This is helpful when sewing plaids or designs that must match up in long seams. Use on heavy, bulky, or quilted fabrics as with insulated shades or quilted placemats.

Bias tape maker uniformly folds the raw edges of fabric strips as you press. Use it to make bias binding for placemats or table runners, or custom band trims on curtains or tablecloths. Tape makers come in four sizes to make folded strips: ½", ¾", 1", or 2" (1.3, 2, 2.5, or 5 cm).

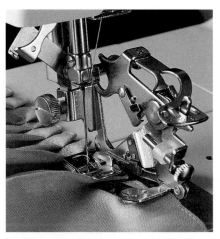

Ruffler attachment automatically gathers strips of light or medium-weight fabric, with adjustments for fullness and tuck frequency. The attachment can be set to gather or tuck a single strip or gather a top strip while attaching it to an underlayer. Use this attachment to make ruffles for curtains, pillows, or dust ruffles.

Serger Features

Sergers can make fast work of some tasks that are more tedious when sewn with a conventional sewing machine. They can accomplish in one pass what may take two or three passes on a conventional machine plus hand trimming work. Refer to your owner's manual for specific information on stitch settings for the various serger tasks.

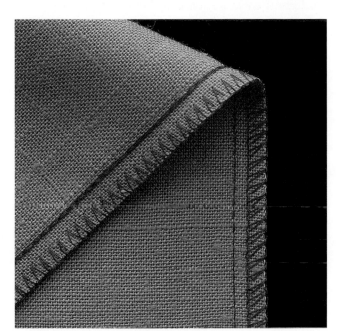

4-Thread or 5-thread safety stitch quickly and securely stitches long seams while trimming the seam allowances to a uniform width and overcasting the raw edges together. Use this stitch for seams on curtains and draperies or any other seams when the seam allowances will be pressed to one side.

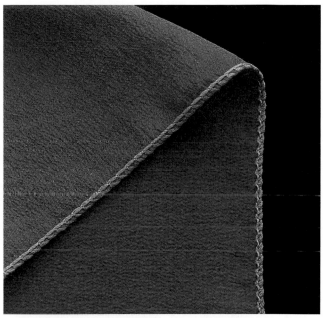

Rolled hem stitch forms neat narrow hems with little effort on the part of the sewer. Use it for hemming long edges on ruffles or for a neat edge finish on fine table linens.

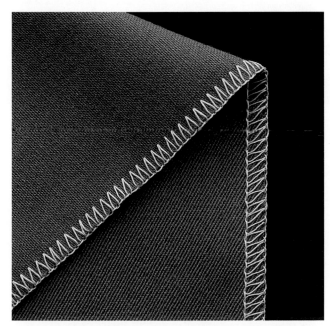

Overedge stitch. Use a short, balanced 2-thread or 3-thread overedge stitch to make a neat, decorative edge finish on napkins or tablecloths. Use this stitch slightly longer as a secure finish for seam allowances that are pressed open.

Differential feed, available on most sergers, offers many options. At its highest differential feed setting, the serger will gather a strip of fabric to about double fullness while overcasting the edge. This feature is useful for making instant curtain ruffles or dust ruffles.

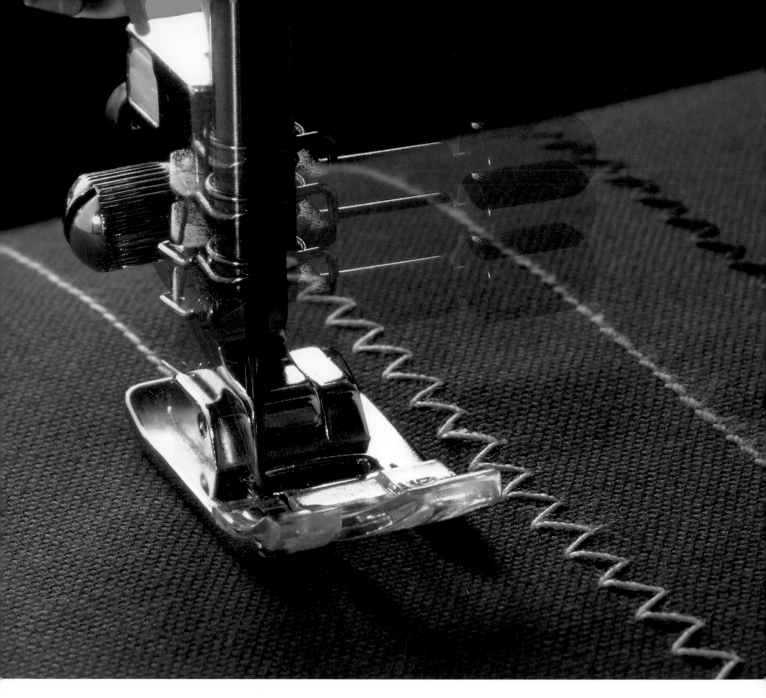

Machine Stitching

Most home decorator sewing can be done entirely by machine with a straight or zigzag stitch. Although machines vary in capabilities, each has the same basic parts and controls. Consult your machine manual to review the threading procedures and to locate the controls that operate the principal parts.

Tension, pressure, and stitch length and width are the main adjustments that create perfect straight or zigzag stitching. Choosing the appropriate needle and thread for the sewing project and fabric also helps to create quality stitching.

Tension is the balance between the upper and bobbin threads as they pass through the machine.

When tension is perfectly balanced, the stitches look even on both sides of the fabric because they link midway between fabric layers. Tension that is too tight causes seams to pucker and stitches to break easily. Tension that is too loose results in weak seams.

Pressure regulates the even feeding of fabric layers. When pressure is too heavy, the bottom fabric layer gathers, forcing the upper layer ahead of the presser foot. This unevenness can make a difference of several inches at the end of a long seam, such as one on a curtain. Pressure that is too light may cause skipped stitches, crooked stitching lines, and weak, loose stitches.

Stitch length is controlled with a regulator that is on an inch scale from 0 to 20, a metric scale from 0 to 4, or a numerical scale from 0 to 9. On the metric and numerical scales, higher numbers form a longer stitch, lower numbers a shorter stitch. For normal stitching, set the regulator at 10 to 12 stitches per inch (2.5 cm). This setting is equivalent to 2.5 to 2 on the metric scale, and 5 on the numerical scale.

Needle, size 11/80, is used for general-purpose sewing on mediumweight fabrics. Because the firm weave and glazed finish of many home decorator fabrics dull a needle quickly, change the needle often. A bent, blunt, or burred needle damages fabric. Prevent damage to the needle by removing pins from the seam as you come to them. Never sew over pins or let them get under the fabric where they may come in contact with the feed dogs.

Thread for general-purpose sewing is suitable for most home decorator projects. Use an all-purpose weight. Choose all-polyester or cotton-wrapped polyester thread that matches or blends with the fabric. For balanced tension, use the same type of thread in the bobbin and the needle.

Thread the machine correctly; incorrect threading can cause a stitch to be too loose or too tight. To rethread the machine, remove the spool completely and begin again, in case the thread has tangled in the tension or over the spool pin.

Use a scrap of fabric to test the tension, pressure, and stitch length before starting to sew. To check the balance of the tension, you may want to thread the machine with different colors for upper and bobbin threads so the stitches are easier to see.

Perfect Straight & Zigzag Stitching

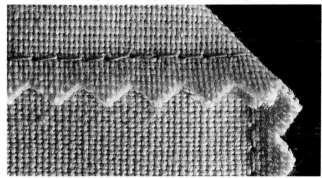

Straight stitches should link midway between fabric layers so stitches are the same length on both sides of fabric. Adjust tension and pressure so stitches do not break easily and the seam does not pucker.

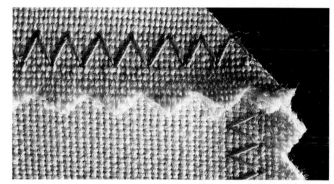

Zigzag stitching is adjusted correctly when the links interlock at the corner of each stitch. Stitches should lie flat. Adjust the zigzag width and density with the stitch length and width regulators.

Machine Stitching Terms

Bastestitching (a) is the longest straight stitch on the machine: 6 on the inch scale, 4 on the metric scale, and 9 on the numerical scale. Some sewing machines have a separate built-in bastestitch **(b)** that makes two stitches to the inch (2.5 cm). Use it for speed-basting straight seams.

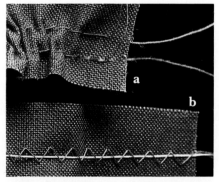

Gathering stitch is done with two rows of bastestitching placed ½" (1.3 cm) and ¼" (6 mm) from the fabric edge. Loosen tension, use heavier bobbin thread, and pull up bobbin thread to form gathers **(a)**. For long areas of gathers, zigzag over cord, string, or dental floss without catching cord in the stitch **(b).** Pull up cord to gather.

Edgestitching is placed on the edge of a hem or fold. The straight-stitch foot and straight-stitch needle plate aid in the close control needed for this stitching. The narrow foot rides on the folded edge, and the small hole of the needle plate keeps fragile fabric from being drawn into the feed dogs.

Basic Seams

All seams in home decor sewing are ½" (1.3 cm) unless otherwise specified. To secure straight seams, backstitch a few stitches at each end. For most projects, avoid using the selvage as a seam allowance edge. Though this tightly woven, nonraveling edge would eliminate the need for extra finishing, it will make the seam allowance pucker and may shrink excessively when steamed or laundered. The exception to this rule is stitching long seams in loosely woven fabrics like casements or laces.

Long seams tend to pucker in some fabrics, especially sheers. To prevent this, practice taut sewing. As you sew, pull equally on the fabric in front and back of the needle as if the fabric were in an embroidery hoop. Do not stretch. Pull the fabric taut, and let it feed through the machine on its own.

The following seams are the most commonly used seams for home decorator sewing.

Plain seam, pressed open, is suitable for almost every fabric and application when you plan to enclose the seam or cover it with lining. If the seam allowances will be exposed or if the item will be laundered often, finish the seam allowances with a zigzag or overlock with a serger.

Plain seam, pressed to one side, is most commonly used for curtains. The seam allowances are pressed toward the return edge of the curtain. Finish the seam allowance edges together, especially if the item will not be lined or if the fabric tends to ravel.

4-Thread or 5-thread safety stitch on a serger trims the seam allowances to a uniform width while stitching a seam and overcasting the seam allowances together. Use this stitch for curtains or any item where the seam allowances are exposed.

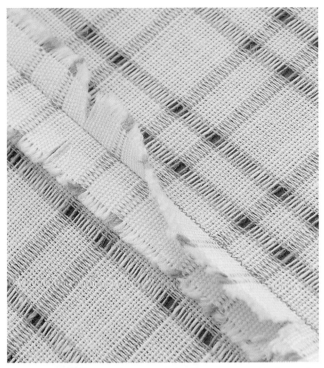

Narrow zigzag stitch is used for long seams in loosely woven fabrics or laces. The zigzag allows the seam to relax slightly and prevents puckers. If removing the selvage would cause excessive raveling, leave the selvages on and clip them up to the stitching line every 1" to 6" (2.5 to 15 cm) to allow them to relax.

French seam eliminates raw edges by encasing them. It is especially suitable for lightweight, sheer, and loosely woven fabrics when the item will be laundered or exposed to abrasion.

How to Sew a French Seam

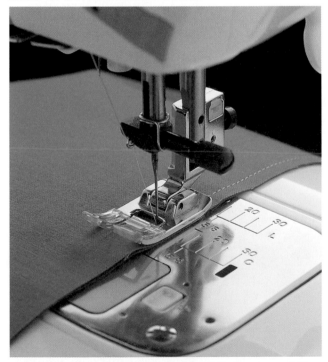

1) Pin fabric *wrong* sides together. Stitch a scant ¼" (6 mm) seam. Trim seam allowance edges to remove any fraying ends. Press seam allowances to one side.

2) Turn fabric panels right sides together, enclosing trimmed seam allowance. Stitching line should be exactly on fold. Stitch ¼" (6 mm) from folded edge, enclosing first seam. Press seam to one side.

Hand Stitching

Almost all sewing for home decorator projects can be done on the machine, but sometimes hand stitching is necessary. Closing seam openings on pillows, attaching trims, and finishing hems are tasks which may require delicate hand sewing.

To make hand stitching easier, run the thread through beeswax to make it stronger and prevent it from snarling. Use a long needle for the running stitch. Hemming and tacking are usually easier with a short needle.

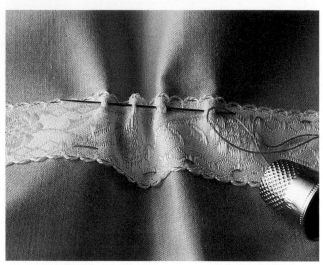

Running stitch is a straight stitch used for temporary basting, easing, gathering, or stitching seams. Work from right to left, taking several stitches onto needle before pulling it through. For easing or gathering or for seams, make stitches ⅛" to ¼" (3 to 6 mm) long. For basting, make stitches ½" to ¾" (1.3 to 2 cm) long; use longer stitches for speed-basting.

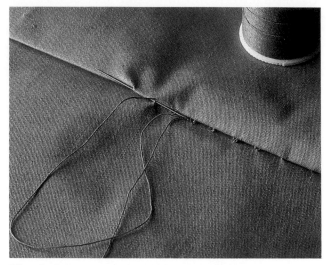

Slipstitch is a nearly invisible stitch for hems, seam openings, linings, or trims. Work from right to left, holding folded edge in left hand. Bring needle up through fold and pull thread through. Then take a tiny stitch in body of fabric, directly opposite point where thread came out. Continue taking stitches every ¼" (6 mm).

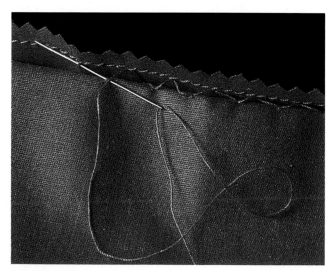

Blindstitch makes a hem that is inconspicuous from either side. Work from right to left with needle pointing left. Take a tiny stitch in body of fabric. Roll hem edge back slightly and take next stitch in underside of hem, ¼" to ½" (6 mm to 1.3 cm) to left of first stitch. Do not pull thread too tightly.

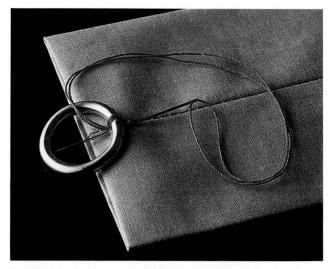

Tacking is used to attach rings and weights, secure linings, or hold facings in place. Using double thread, take two or three stitches in the same place, one on top of the other. Secure with a backstitch. When tacking through more than one layer of fabric, do not sew through to outside layer.

Padded Work Surface

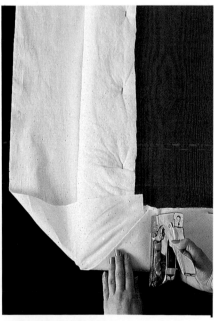

Make a padded work surface to lay out an entire panel for cutting, measuring, squaring off ends, and pressing. The square corners and ample width make it easier to work with square and rectangular shapes. Fabric does not slide on the muslin-covered surface; you can also pin into it and press directly on it.

For small projects, use the *square* end of a regular ironing board as a work surface.

Use a steam-spray iron for all your pressing needs. To press fabric, lift and lower the iron in one place. This up-and-down motion prevents fabrics from stretching or distorting. Let the steam do the work. To make sharp creases or to smooth a stubborn wrinkle, spray the fabric with water or spray sizing.

YOU WILL NEED

Hollow door or ¾" (2 cm) plywood, approximately 3' × 7' (.95 × 2.16 m), set on saw horses.

Padding, cotton batting (not polyester), table pads, or blankets, ¼" to ½" (6 mm to 1.3 cm) thick, enough to overlap door or plywood 6" (15 cm) on all sides.

Muslin or unpatterned sheet, approximately 6" (15 cm) larger than door or plywood on all sides.

How to Make a Padded Work Surface

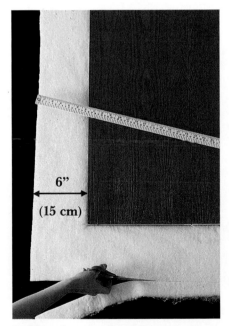

1) Place layers of padding on the floor or on a large, flat surface. Center the door on top of the padding; cut padding 6" (15 cm) larger than the door on all sides.

2) Fold padding over one long edge of the door and tack with 4 or 5 staples. Pull padding on opposite edge and tack. Repeat on both ends. Secure with staples 3" (7.5 cm) apart.

3) Center padded door on top of muslin. Wrap and fasten with staples 3" (7.5 cm) apart. Turn right side up and spray muslin with water. As it dries, muslin shrinks slightly so cover fits tightly.

Windows

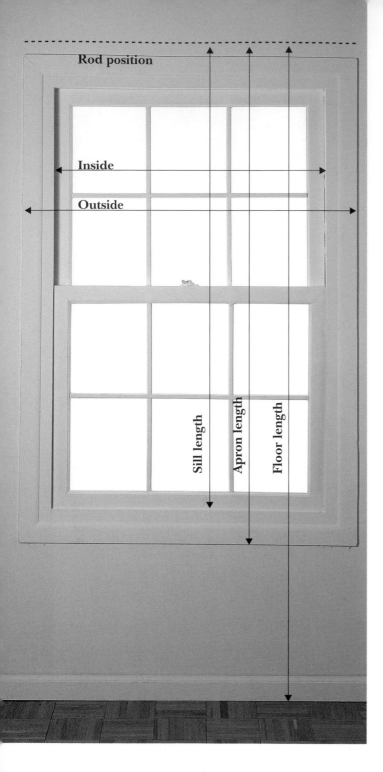

Rod position

Inside

Outside

Sill length

Apron length

Floor length

Window Fashions

Measuring the Window

Before measuring windows, select the style of curtain, drapery, or shade you will make. The style of window treatment determines what installation hardware is necessary. Next, decide exactly where the window treatment will be placed; install the hardware and measure this area for the finished size of the curtain, shade, or drapery.

Curtain rods may be attached to the window frame, within or at the sides of the frame, on the wall above the frame, or at the ceiling.

Mounting boards are necessary for hanging Roman shades and other shades based on the Roman shade construction. These 1 × 2 boards are cut to the width of the shade, stapled or tacked to the shade's upper edge, then installed at the window. An *inside-mounted* shade fits firmly inside the top of the window frame. An *outside-mounted* shade is installed on the wall above the frame. A *hybrid-mounted* shade is a combination mount. The mounting board is placed inside the window, but the shade extends over part of the window frame.

Roller shades are installed inside or on the window frame, or on the wall above.

Follow these guidelines for accurate measuring:

• Use a folding ruler or metal tape for measuring; cloth tapes may stretch or sag.

• Measure and record the measurements for all windows separately, even if they *appear* to be the same size. Size differences, even if slight, should be taken into account when constructing window treatments.

• When measuring for a shade that fits inside the window, measure the window width at the top, center, and bottom to determine if it is true and square.

• When measuring for curtains on a window without an apron, measure to at least 4" (10 cm) below the sill.

Window Measurements for Curtains, Shades, and Draperies

Treatment	Finished Length	Finished Width
Curtains	Measure from top of rod or heading to desired length (sill, apron, or floor).	Measure rod from end to end, plus *returns* (short ends of the rod that stand out from the wall).
Roller Shades	Measure from top of roller to sill.	Measure length of roller.
Other Shades	Measure from top of mounting board to sill or desired length.	Measure mounting board from end to end.
Valances	Measure from top of heading to desired length (about ⅓ distance from top to floor).	Measure rod from end to end plus returns.
Use these measurements with chart (page 25) to estimate amount of fabric needed.		

Estimating Yardage

Because fabric widths vary, yardage cannot be figured until the fabric has been selected. After you have taken the necessary measurements and determined the finished size of the curtain, shade, or drapery, you must add to the length and width for seams, hems, headings, and fullness. This is the *cut length*. Use the cut length to estimate the amount of fabric you will need. For curtains and draperies, use the amounts as listed below and transfer the correct amount to the chart (right). For shade yardage, see individual instructions for each type of shade.

Determining Length

To the *finished length*, add the amount needed for lower hems, rod pockets, headings, and pattern repeat.

Lower hems. Add double the desired hem to the finished length. For mediumweight fabrics, use a 4" (10 cm) double-fold hem on floor-length curtains or draperies; add 8" (20.5 cm) to the length. Or on short curtains or valances, use a 1" to 3" (2.5 to 7.5 cm) double-fold hem; add 2" to 6" (5 to 15 cm) to the length. For sheer and lightweight fabrics, a deeper double-fold hem of 5" to 6" (12.5 to 15 cm) may be used; add 10" to 12" (25.5 to 30.5 cm) to the length.

Rod pockets and headings. For simple rod pockets with no heading, add an amount equal to the diameter of the rod plus ½" (1.3 cm) to turn under and ¼" to 1" (6 mm to 2.5 cm) ease. The amount of ease depends on the size of the rod and thickness of the fabric. Lightweight fabrics require less ease; rod pockets for large rods require more. For rod pockets with headings, use the formula for a simple rod pocket, adding to it an amount twice the depth of the heading.

Pattern repeat. Fabrics with patterns (motifs) need to be matched. Measure the distance between motifs and add that amount to the length of each panel.

Determining Width

To the *finished width*, add the amount needed for seams, side hems, and fullness.

Seams. For multi-width panels, add 1" (2.5 cm) for each seam. Panels that are not wider than the fabric do not require an extra amount for seams.

Side hems. Add 6" (15 cm) per panel for a 1½" (3.8 cm) double-fold hem on each side of the panel.

Fullness. Fabric weight determines fullness. For medium to heavyweight fabrics, add two to two-and-one-half times the finished width of the curtain. For sheer and lightweight fabrics, add two-and-one-half to three times the finished width.

Make a copy of this chart and fill it in to help you figure the correct amount of fabric needed for curtains, shades, or draperies.

Figuring Yardage

Cut Length	in. (cm)
For fabrics not requiring pattern match:	
1) Finished length	
2) Bottom hem (double for most fabrics) +	
3) Rod pocket/heading +	
4) Cut length for each width or part width =	
For fabrics requiring pattern match:	
1) Cut length (figure as above)	
2) Size of pattern repeat (distance between motifs) ÷	
3) Number of repeats needed* =	
4) Cut length for each width or part width: multiply size of repeat by number of repeats needed	

Cut Width	
1) Finished length	
2) Fullness (how many times the finished width) ×	
3) Width times fullness =	
4) Side hems +	
5) Total width needed =	
6) Width of fabric	
7) Number of fabric widths: total width needed divided by width of fabric*	

Total Fabric Needed		
1) Cut length (as figured above)		
2) Number of fabric widths (as figured above)	×	
3) Total fabric length	=	
4) Number of yds. (meters) needed: total fabric length divided by 36" (100 cm)	yds. (m)	

*Round up to the nearest whole number.

NOTE: Add extra fabric for straightening ends.

NOTE: Half of the width (determined above) will be used for each curtain panel. To piece panels, adjust width measurement to include 1" (2.5 cm) for each seam.

Cutting & Matching

Cut fabric on the true crosswise grain to *square* the ends. Squaring ensures that curtains will always hang straight. Some fabrics can be squared by pulling a yarn on the crosswise grain and cutting along the space.

Avoid prints that are obviously off-grain. If these fabrics are cut on-grain, the design motif will be crooked and impossible to match at seams and edges. Many prints and woven patterns are only slightly off-grain, but their unevenness may be more apparent once the curtains are hung. Square the ends of these fabrics by cutting on a line of the design rather than on the crosswise grain.

Some decorator fabrics have a permanent finish which holds the threads in place. Chintz, polished cotton, and other permanent-finish fabrics can be squared by simply cutting straight across the ends.

To obtain the desired finished curtain width, you may need to seam several widths of fabric together. Match the design motif of the fabric carefully so that seams are as inconspicuous as possible.

Three Ways to Straighten Crosswise Ends

Pull one or two yarns across the width of the fabric, from selvage to selvage. Cut on the line that appears after yarns have been pulled out.

Use a carpenter's square to straighten fabrics that have a permanent finish. Place one side of square parallel to selvage. Mark along other side of square; cut on marked line. Or align selvage to corner of table; cut across end.

Locate a design that runs straight across the fabric on the crosswise grain. Cut along the design. Consider depth of hem or heading when determining placement of the design on the finished curtain.

How to Match Design Motifs

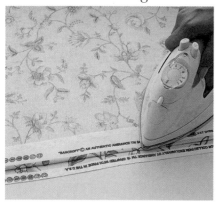

1) **Position** fabric widths right sides together, matching selvages. Fold back upper selvage until pattern matches; press foldline.

2) **Unfold** selvage, and pin the fabric widths together on foldline. Check the match from right side.

3) **Repin** the fabric so the pins are perpendicular to foldline; stitch on the foldline, using straight stitch. Trim off selvages evenly, leaving ½" (1.3 cm) seam allowances.

Hemming

If you have measured, figured, and cut accurately, your curtains should fit windows perfectly once they are hemmed. For the neatest and easiest hems, follow the procedure used in professional workrooms: sew the lower hems first, the side hems next, and rod pockets and headings last.

Side and lower hems of curtains are always double to provide strength, weight, and stability. The most accurate way to make a double-fold hem is to press the full hem depth under first, and then turn the cut edge under up to the foldline. Cut off the selvages evenly before pressing the side hems.

Curtains hang better when hems are weighted or anchored. Sew small weights into the hems at the lower corners and bottoms of seams to keep the curtain from pulling or puckering. Use heavier weights for full-length curtains, lighter weights for lightweight fabrics and shorter curtains.

How to Sew Double-fold Hems

Lower hem. 1) Turn under and press the full hem allowance on the lower edge; 8" (20.5 cm) for floor-length curtains or 6" (15 cm) for sill-length curtains. Unfold and turn cut edge under to meet foldline; press outer fold.

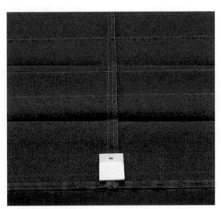

2) Tack drapery weight to hem allowance at each seam. Refold on inner foldline, encasing cut edge; pin. Stitch hem.

Side hems. Turn under and press 1½" (3.8 cm) double-fold side hems as in step 1 for lower hem; pin. Tack drapery weights inside hems, about 3" (7.5 cm) from lower edge. Refold and stitch hem.

Three Ways to Finish Curtain Hems

Straight-stitch on folded hem edge, using 8 to 10 stitches per inch (2.5 cm). Use thread to match solid color fabric or blend with multicolor fabric. Stitch slowly through multiple layers.

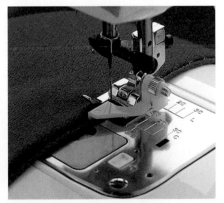

Machine blindstitch. Adjust machine to blindstitch setting and attach blindstitch foot. Fold hem under, leaving inner fold extending ⅛" (3 mm). Align guide in foot to soft fold. Adjust stitch width to take tiny bite into soft fold.

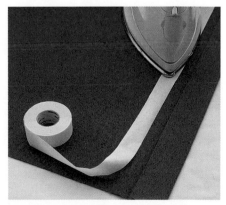

Fused hem. Fuse paper-backed fusible web to hem; remove paper backing, and fuse hem in place. Follow manufacturer's instructions for fusing. Press from both sides.

Curtains

Curtains are a traditional favorite for window fashions. They are flat, nonpleated panels, so they are easier to clean and press than many other window treatments.

Curtains are often made of lightweight or sheer fabrics. Heavier fabrics such as linen, chintz, or textured or polished cotton look best for formal, floor-length curtains. Lighter, crisper fabrics work well for casual, sill-length, and cafe curtains. Sheer curtains are usually two-and-one-half to three times the fullness of the finished width; heavier fabrics require only double fullness.

Mount curtains at windows on stationary rods or poles. Choose 1", 2½", or 4" (2.5, 6.5, or 10 cm) utility rods or plain wooden poles if they will be completely covered by the fabric. Select decorative metal or wooden poles if part of the pole will be exposed.

Rod pockets are channels stitched in place along the upper edge of curtains. The rod pockets are open at both ends so a curtain rod or pole can be inserted.

Headings are optional on curtains. The heading creates a decorative ruffle above the rod pocket along the upper edge of the curtain.

Linings add weight and body to curtains. Although a lining may not be necessary, it can improve a curtain's appearance and give it a custom look.

Tab-top curtains have fabric loops instead of a rod pocket along the upper edge. These curtains are used with decorative metal or wooden poles.

Ruffled curtains have a graceful appearance. Ruffles add weight to curtains and make them hang and drape more attractively.

Tiebacks are separate fabric strips which hold curtains open and emphasize the drape of the curtain. Tiebacks can be straight, shaped, or ruffled and are used for stationary curtain panels.

Rod-pocket Styles for Curtains

Simple rod pocket is stitched along the upper edge of the curtain. It may be used for sheer curtains that hang behind draperies, a valance, or cornice.

Heading creates a ruffled edge above rod pocket. Headings are from 1" to 5" (2.5 to 12.5 cm) deep, depending on curtain length and weight of the fabric.

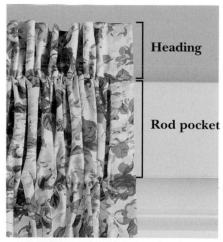

Wide rod pocket and heading are used with a 2½" or 4" (6.5 or 10 cm) rod. They are well suited for floor-length curtains, where rod pocket and heading depth should balance with curtain length.

Rod Pockets & Headings

A rod pocket is the channel along the upper edge of the curtain or valance. The curtain rod is inserted through the rod pocket so that the fullness of the curtain falls into soft gathers.

Before cutting the curtains, decide on the rod-pocket style. A simple rod pocket places the curtain rod at the uppermost edge of the curtain.

For simple rod pockets, measure around the widest part of the rod or pole; add ½" (1.3 cm) ease to this measurement and divide by two. Also add ½" (1.3 cm) to turn under.

A heading is a gathered edge above the rod pocket. It finishes the curtain more decoratively than a simple rod pocket. Curtains with headings do not require cornices or valances.

For rod pockets with headings, use the formula for a simple rod pocket, adding to it an amount twice the

depth of the heading. Headings may be from 1" to 5" (2.5 to 12.5 cm) deep. The depth of the heading must be determined before the curtains are cut. The heading depth should be appropriate for the length of the curtain: in general, the longer the curtain, the deeper the heading.

Wooden, brass, or plastic poles may be covered with a *shirred pole cover*. The exposed pole between the curtain panels is covered with a rod pocket made from a shirred tube of matching fabric (above). The rod pocket may be plain or have a heading the same height as the curtain heading. Wide poles and rod pockets are more than decorative. They often are used to conceal a shade heading, the plain heading on shirred curtains, or the traverse rod of sheer or lightweight curtains.

Finish lower and side hems of curtains before sewing rod pockets and headings.

How to Sew a Simple Rod Pocket

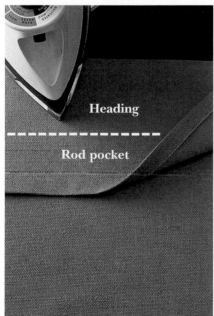

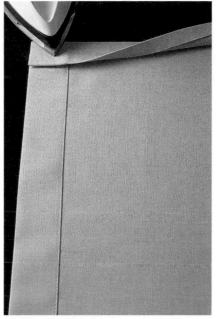

1) Determine rod-pocket depth by loosely pinning a curtain fabric strip around the rod. Remove rod and measure the distance from the top of the strip to the pin. Add ½" (1.3 cm) to be turned under.

2) Press under ½" (1.3 cm) along upper cut edge of curtain panel. Fold over again at the rod-pocket depth; press.

3) Stitch close to inner folded edge to form rod pocket, backstitching at both ends. If desired, stitch again close to the upper edge to create a sharp crease appropriate for flat or oval curtain rods.

How to Sew a Rod Pocket with a Heading

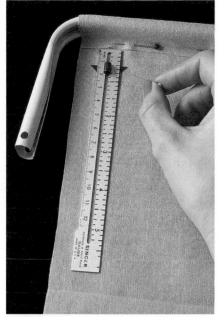

Heading

Rod pocket

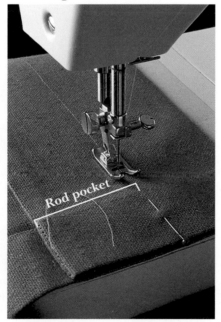

Rod pocket

1) Determine the depth of the rod pocket as directed in step 1, above. Determine the depth of heading, opposite. Press under ½" (1.3 cm) along upper cut edge of the curtain panel. Fold and press again to form hem equal to rod pocket plus heading depth.

2) Stitch close to folded edge, backstitching at both ends. Mark heading depth with a pin at each end of panel. Stitch again at marked depth. To aid straight stitching, apply a strip of masking tape to the bed of the machine at heading depth, or use seam guide.

3) Insert rod through pocket and gather curtain evenly onto rod. Adjust heading by pulling up the folded edge so the seam is exactly on the lower edge of the rod. A wide heading may be made to look puffy and more rounded by pulling the fabric out on each side.

How to Make a Shirred Pole Cover

1) Cut fabric two-and-one-half times the length of the pole area to be covered; cut width equal to circumference of pole plus 1½" (3.8 cm). For pole with a heading, add amount equal to twice the heading depth.

2) Stitch narrow double-fold hems on short ends. Fold strip in half lengthwise, right sides together, and pin long edges together. Stitch ½" (1.3 cm) seam. Press seam open. Turn cover right side out.

3) Press cover so that seam is at back of pole. To form heading, stitch again at appropriate distance from upper folded edge. If desired, add narrow contrasting binding to upper edge (below). Gather pole cover onto rod.

Contrasting binding. 1) Cut 2½" (6.5 cm) strip of fabric with length equal to finished width of panel plus 1" (2.5 cm); seam as necessary, using diagonal seams to reduce bulk. Press under scant ½" (1.3 cm) on one long side and each short end.

2) Pin unpressed edge to upper edge of curtain, right sides together; stitch ½" (1.3 cm) from edge. Press folded edge of binding over upper edge. Stitch in the ditch from the right side.

Lining Rod-pocket Curtains

Lining adds body and weight to curtains. It extends into the heading to keep the ruffled edge from drooping and extends into the side hems for firmer edges that hang well. A lining also adds opaqueness, prevents fading and sun damage to curtain fabric, and provides some insulation. White or off-white cotton drapery lining is manufactured in the same widths as decorator fabrics. A stain-resistant finish makes the lining more durable. Black-out lining is also available for completely blocking sunlight.

✂ Cutting Directions

Cut the lining 5" (12.5 cm) shorter than the cut length of the decorator fabric; this allows for a 2" (5 cm) double-fold hem at the lower edge and for the lining to be 1" (2.5 cm) shorter than the curtain when it is finished. The cut width of the lining is equal to the cut width of the decorator fabric.

How to Sew Lined Rod-pocket Curtains

1) Seam decorator fabric widths, if necessary, for each curtain panel; repeat for lining panel. At lower edge of curtain panel, press under 4" (10 cm) twice to wrong side; stitch to make double-fold hem. Repeat for hem on lining panel, pressing under 2" (5 cm) twice.

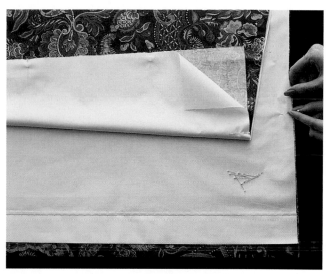

2) Place curtain panel and lining panel wrong sides together, matching raw edges at sides and upper edge; pin. At the bottom, the lining panel will be 1" (2.5 cm) shorter than curtain panel.

3) Press under 1½" (3.8 cm) twice on sides, folding lining and curtain panel as one fabric. Tack drapery weights inside the side hems, about 3" (7.5 cm) from lower edge. Stitch to make double-fold hems, using blindstitch or straight stitch.

4) Press and stitch rod pocket and heading as in steps 1 and 2 at the bottom of page 31; lining and curtain panels are folded as one fabric. Insert pole or rod through rod pocket, gathering fabric evenly. Install pole on brackets.

Ruffled Curtains

Ruffled curtains add a charming, warm touch to any room, and the weight of the ruffles helps curtains hang better. The ruffle on the curtain usually extends from the top of the heading down one side of the panel and across the bottom up to the side hem. If the treatment has two panels that meet in the center, the ruffle on the underlying panel starts just under the rod pocket. Ruffles may be single layer with a finished outer edge or self-faced. For added frill, a narrow ruffle may be applied over a wider ruffle. The curtains may be lined or unlined.

✂ Cutting Directions

Determine the desired finished length of the curtain, from the top of the heading to the lower edge of the ruffle. Cut the fabric for each curtain panel with the cut length equal to the desired finished length of the curtain minus the finished width of the ruffle plus the depth of the heading and rod pocket plus 1" (2.5 cm) for seam allowance and turn-under.

Determine the cut width of each curtain panel by multiplying the length of the rod times the desired fullness; divide this number by the number of panels being used for the treatment, and add 3½" (9 cm) for each panel to allow for a 1½" (3.8 cm) double-fold hem on the return side of the panel plus ½" (1.3 cm) for the seam on the ruffled side.

Cut lining, if desired, to the same length and width as the decorator fabric.

Cut ruffle strips from crosswise grain of fabric. Piece strips together to the necessary length, allowing two to two-and-one-half times fullness; use French seams (page 19) for single-layer ruffles or ¼" (6 mm) plain seams pressed open for self-faced ruffles. For single-layer ruffles, allow ½" (1.3 cm) for seam allowance plus any necessary hem allowance on outer edge. For self-faced ruffles, cut ruffle strips twice the desired finished width plus 1" (2.5 cm) for seam allowances.

How to Make Unlined Ruffled Curtains

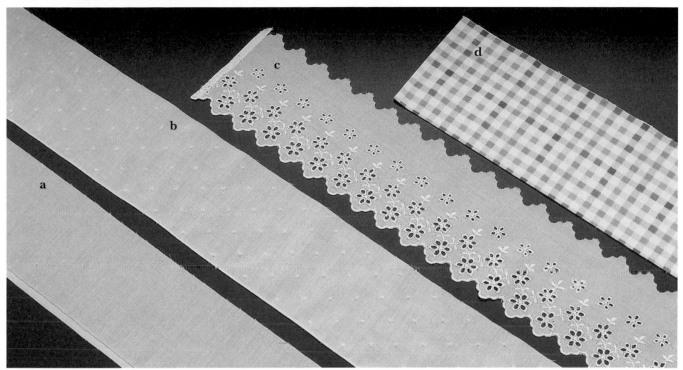

1) Finish outer edge of single-layer ruffle strip with ¼" (6 mm) double-fold hem **(a),** rolled hem sewn on a serger (page 15) **(b),** or select an eyelet trim with finished outer edge **(c).** Finish narrow ends with ¼" (6 mm) double-fold hems. For self-faced ruffles, fold ends of pieced ruffle strip in half, right sides together; stitch across ends in ¼" (6 mm) seam. Turn right side out. Press entire strip in half **(d).**

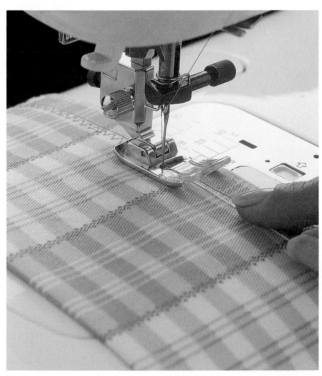

2) Machine-baste layers together ⅜" (1 cm) from raw edges, if making curtains with two layers of ruffles. Zigzag over a cord, such as crochet cotton or dental floss, on back side of ruffle within ½" (1.3 cm) seam allowance. Stitch through both layers of self-faced ruffle.

3) Seam fabric widths together for curtain. Round the lower corner of curtain panels where the ruffle will be applied.

(Continued on next page)

4) Press under ½" (1.3 cm) on upper edge of curtain. Then press under an amount equal to rod-pocket depth plus heading depth. If you are making a panel with ruffle beginning below rod pocket, pin-mark location of lower stitching line for rod pocket. Unfold.

5) Divide curtain edge into equal segments, beginning at top of heading **(a)** or at lower stitching line of rod pocket **(b)** and ending on lower edge 3" (7.5 cm) from raw edge on return side of panel; mark. Divide ruffle strip into same number of segments. Pin ruffle to curtain, right sides together, matching marks and raw edges.

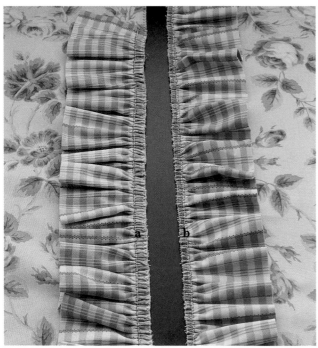

6) Pull gathering cord on ruffle to fit edge of curtain, distributing fullness evenly; pin in place. Stitch ½" (1.3 cm) from edges. Finish edges together, using zigzag **(a).** Or stitch seam and finish edges at once, using 4-thread or 5-thread safety stitch on serger **(b).**

7) Press seam allowances toward curtain. Topstitch on curtain side ¼" (6 mm) from seam so ruffle will lie smooth and even. Press under 1½" (3.8 cm) double-fold side hem; stitch. Refold heading and rod pocket; stitch.

How to Make Lined Ruffled Curtains

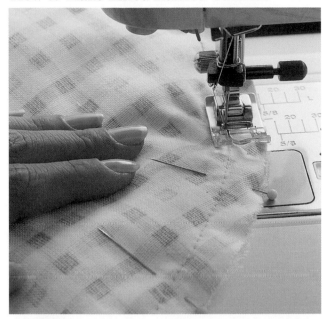

1) **Follow** steps 1 to 3 for unlined curtain on page 35. Round lower corner of lining panels, using curtain panels as guide. Follow steps 4 to 6, but omit seam finish. Pin lining and curtain right sides together along ruffled edges. With curtain side up, stitch seam, stitching just inside previous stitching line.

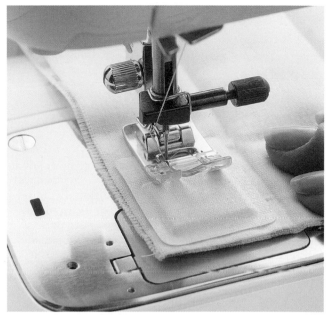

2) **Turn** right side out, matching remaining raw edges of curtain and lining. Press seam. Press under 1½" (3.8 cm) twice on return side of curtain, folding curtain fabric and lining as one. Unfold fabric; tack drapery weight near bottom of hem allowance. Refold; stitch to make double-fold side hem. Refold heading and rod pocket, folding curtain and lining as one; stitch.

Two Timesaving Ways to Make Ruffles

Ruffler attachment. Use a ruffler attachment suitable for your machine to tuck or gather as you sew. Make a test strip and adjust ruffler to desired fullness. Measure the test strip before and after stitching to determine length of fabric needed.

Serger with differential feed. Adjust differential feed for gathering; use shirring foot, if desired. Serge near edge of fabric, trimming slightly. Serger gathers fabric automatically. Make a test strip and adjust differential feed to desired fullness. Measure the test strip before and after stitching to determine length of fabric needed.

Tab-top Curtains

Fabric tabs are an attractive alternative to conventional rod pockets or curtain rings. Tab-top curtains used with a decorative curtain rod create a traditional country look, a contemporary tailored look, or a casual cafe look. They are also ideal for stationary side panels. Tabs give top interest to a curtain and can be made with contrasting fabric, decorative ribbon, or trim.

Only one-and-one-half to two times fullness is needed for tab-top curtains. Allow ½" (1.3 cm) seam allowance at the upper edge of the curtain instead of the usual rod-pocket allowance. When determining the finished length, allow for the upper edge of the curtain to be 1½" to 2" (3.8 to 5 cm) below the rod. This determines the length of the tabs. Determine the number of tabs needed by placing a tab at each edge of the curtain, and space the remaining tabs 6" to 8" (15 to 20.5 cm) apart.

How to Sew Tab-top Curtains

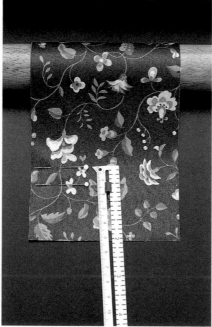

1) Cut a 3" (7.5 cm) facing strip equal in length to the width of the curtain panel. Press under ½" (1.3 cm) on one long side and each short end. Press double-fold lower and side hems of curtain. Stitch lower hem only.

2) Measure tab length by pinning a strip of fabric over the rod and marking the desired length with a pin. Add ½" (1.3 cm) for seam allowance. Cut tabs to measured length, and two times the desired width plus 1" (2.5 cm).

3) Fold each tab in half lengthwise, right sides together. Stitch ½" (1.3 cm) seam along cut edge; sew from one tab to the next, using continuous stitching. Turn tabs right side out. Center seam in back of each tab; press.

4) Fold each tab in half so raw edges are aligned. Pin or baste tabs in place on right side of curtain, aligning raw edges of tabs with upper edge of curtain. Place end tabs even with side hem foldline of curtain.

5) Pin facing to upper edge of curtain, right sides together, so raw edges are aligned and tabs are sandwiched between facing and curtain. Stitch ½" (1.3 cm) seam, with curtain side hems extended.

6) Press facing to wrong side of curtain so tabs extend upward. Fold curtain side hems under facing, covering seam allowance; grade. Stitch side hems. Slipstitch facing to curtain. Insert curtain rod through tabs.

Tiebacks

Tiebacks are a decorative way to hold curtains open. Make them straight or shaped, ruffled or plain. Use matching or contrasting solids, coordinating prints, or bordered fabrics. Interface all tiebacks to add stability.

An easy way to make tiebacks the proper length is to complete and hang the curtains before sewing the tiebacks. Cut a strip of fabric that is 2" to 4" (5 to 10 cm) wide; experiment by pinning it around the curtains to determine the best tieback length. Slide the strip up and down to find the best location for tiebacks. Mark the wall for positioning tieback holders, which will be used to fasten the tiebacks. Remove the strip and measure it to determine the finished size.

✂ Cutting Directions

For straight tiebacks, cut a piece of heavyweight fusible interfacing the finished length and two times the finished width. To cut fabric, add ½" (1.3 cm) on all sides for seams.

For shaped tiebacks, cut a strip of brown paper for pattern, 4" to 6" (10 to 15 cm) wide and slightly longer than the tieback. Pin the paper around the curtain and draw a curved shape around the edge of the paper. Experiment by pinning and trimming the paper to get the effect you want. Cut two pieces of fabric and heavyweight fusible interfacing for each tieback. Cut interfacing same size as pattern. To cut fabric, add ½" (1.3 cm) on all sides for seams.

YOU WILL NEED

Decorator fabric for tiebacks.

Heavyweight fusible interfacing.

Brown paper for pattern.

Fusible web strips, length of finished tieback width.

Two ⅝" (1.5 cm) brass or plastic rings for each tieback.

Two tieback holders.

How to Sew Straight Tiebacks

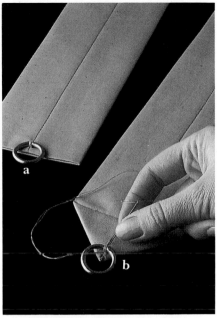

1) Center fusible interfacing on wrong side of tieback and fuse. Press the short ends under ½" (1.3 cm). Fold tieback in half lengthwise, right sides together. Stitch ½" (1.3 cm) seam, leaving short ends open. Press open.

2) Turn tieback right side out. Center seam down back and press. Turn pressed ends inside. Insert fusible web at each end and fuse. Or slipstitch closed.

3) Hand-tack ring on back seamline at each end of tieback, ¼" (6 mm) from edge **(a)**. Or press corners diagonally to inside to form a point; slipstitch or fuse corners in place. Attach ring **(b)**.

How to Sew Shaped Tiebacks

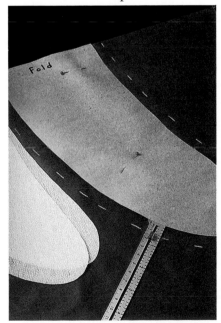

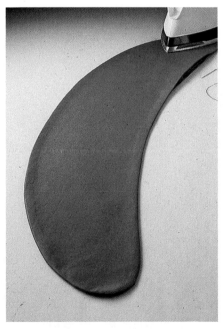

1) Position pattern on fold to cut fabric and interfacing. Center interfacing on wrong side of each tieback piece and fuse.

2) Pin tieback pieces, right sides together. Stitch ½" (1.3 cm) seam, leaving 4" (10 cm) opening on one long edge for turning. Grade seam allowances; notch or clip curves at regular intervals.

3) Turn tieback right side out; press. Insert fusible web at opening and fuse. Or slipstitch closed. Hand-tack rings at each end of tieback ¼" (6 mm) from the edge.

Bound Tiebacks

Binding emphasizes the graceful line of a curved tieback and allows you to pick up an accent color from the room decor or from the curtain fabric. Shaped tiebacks are easier to bind than straight tiebacks because the bias binding will ease around curves.

✂ Cutting Directions

Cut two pieces of fabric and two pieces of fusible interfacing from the pattern; do not add seam allowances to tieback. Make bias tape as on page 72, cutting bias strips 2" (5 cm) wide. Cut the tape 1" (2.5 cm) longer than the distance around the tieback.

How to Bind Shaped Tiebacks

1) Position pattern on fold to cut fabric and interfacing. Fuse interfacing to wrong side of tieback. Pin wrong sides of tieback together.

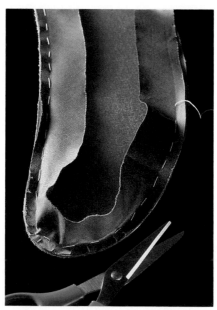

2) Press under ½" (1.3 cm) on one end of bias strip. Starting with pressed end, baste strip to tieback, right sides together, clipping to ease around curves. Stitch strip ½" (1.3 cm) from edge.

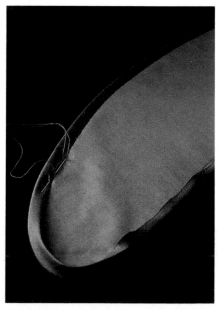

3) Press bias strip over edge of tieback. Turn under cut edge of bias strip so fold meets seamline; slipstitch. Hand-tack rings to ends of tieback.

Ruffled Tiebacks

Adding ruffled tiebacks changes the appearance of the curtains and the look of a window. Make ruffles from a matching or coordinating fabric in a width that suits the length of the curtain. Purchased pregathered lace or eyelet ruffles may be used to reduce sewing time.

✂ Cutting Directions

Cut ruffle the desired width plus 1" (2.5 cm) for seam and hem, and two-and-one-half times the finished length.

Cut a straight tieback and inter-facing (page 40). The tieback should be in proportion to the ruffle width, usually less than half as wide.

How to Sew Ruffled Tiebacks

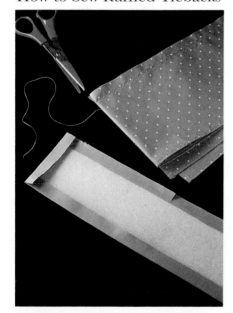

1) Fuse interfacing to wrong side of tieback. Press under ½" (1.3 cm) on one long side and both ends of tie-back. Stitch a ¼" (6 mm) double-fold hem on one long side and both ends of ruffle. Fold ruffle and tieback into fourths; mark folds with snips.

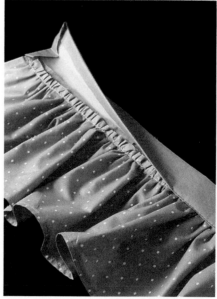

2) Zigzag over a cord (page 35). Pin wrong side of ruffle to right side of tieback, matching snips and raw edges. Pull up gathering cord until ruffle fits tieback. Distribute gathers evenly and pin. Stitch ruffle ½" (1.3 cm) from edge.

3) Fold tieback in half lengthwise, wrong sides together. Pin the folded edge over ruffle seam. Edgestitch across ends and along gathered seam. Hand-tack the rings to ends of tieback.

Easy Pleated Draperies

Pleated draperies are easy to sew with pleater tape, which eliminates tedious, complicated measuring.

Pinch pleats are the traditional pleated heading for draperies. Each pinch pleat is actually three small pleats grouped together at regular intervals. Pleater tape for pinch pleats has evenly spaced pockets woven into it; special four-pronged pleater hooks inserted into the pockets draw up the pleats.

Select pleater tape that gives the desired drapery fullness. Some pleater tapes are designed to give an exact double fullness; others allow for more or less than double fullness, depending on how the pockets are used. Determine the drapery fullness (page 25) according to the fabric weight; lightweight fabrics require more fullness than heavy fabrics.

Panel draperies are stationary pleated panels that hang at the sides of the window.

Draw draperies can be closed to cover the entire width of the window. These draperies hang on traverse rods and pull open to one side only (one-way draw) or to both sides (two-way draw).

Before cutting fabric or tape, prepleat the *tape only* using pleater hooks to determine the finished width of the draperies and the pleat position. Pleat tape to the width of the drapery panel and hang it on the rod. Adjust pleats as necessary so the last pleat of the panel is at the corner of the rod return. Do not position pleats on the return or at the center of two-way draperies where panels overlap. Remove pleater hooks and measure tape to determine the finished width of drapery panels, as in steps 1 and 2, opposite.

✂ Cutting Directions

After pleating tape to correct size, cut pleater tape for each panel so that panels have pockets in the same position. Add ½" (1.3 cm) at each end of pleater tape for finishing.

Cut decorator fabric so width is the length of the pleater tape plus 6" (15 cm) to allow for 1½" (3.8 cm) double-fold side hems. Seam fabric if necessary, allowing 1" (2.5 cm) for each seam. For length, cut fabric finished length, plus 8" (20.5 cm) to allow for 4" (10 cm) double-fold hem and ½" (1.3 cm) for turning under on upper edge.

YOU WILL NEED

Decorator fabric for draperies.

Pleater tape to match style of heading.

Pleater hooks and end pins.

How to Sew Unlined Pinch-pleated Draperies

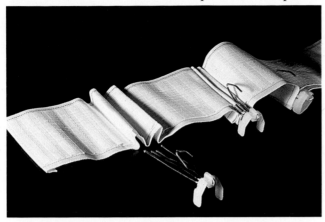

1) Prepleat pleater tape to finished width of drapery panel. Leave space unpleated at one end of tape for overlap and at other end for return.

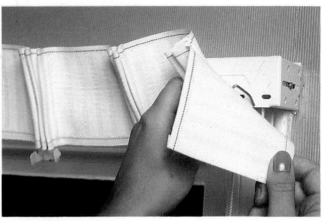

2) Position the pleater tape on installed traverse rod and adjust pleats if necessary. Fold ends under ½" (1.3 cm). Remove hooks. Cut drapery panels using pleater tape as guide.

3) Turn under double-fold hem on lower edge and double-fold hems on sides; stitch. Mark ½" (1.3 cm) from upper edge on right side of drapery.

4) Pin upper edge of pleater tape, pocket side up, along marked line so that pleater tape overlaps drapery ½" (1.3 cm). Stitch ¼" (6 mm) from edge of pleater tape.

5) Fold pleater tape to inside of drapery so it is even with finished upper edge of drapery; press. Stitch lower edge and both sides of tape, following guideline on tape, if marked.

6) Insert hooks. Push prongs all the way up into pleats. Adjust folds between hooks.

Shades

Shades control light and provide privacy when used alone or with curtains. Because they fit close to windows, shades are also energy efficient.

Shades can be mounted either inside or outside the window frame. The screws can be inserted on either the narrow or wide side of the mounting board. This will determine how far from the window your shade will hang.

Roman shade is the basis for stitched-tuck, hobbled, cloud, balloon, and insulated shades. These shades are raised and lowered by a system of cords and rings, which cause them to pleat into soft folds when raised.

Stitched-tuck shade has small, topstitched tucks along the folds of the shade. These tucked rows alternate between the front and the back of the shade, giving the pleats a crisp look.

Hobbled shade is two times the length of a flat Roman shade. Excess fabric is taken up in

permanent soft folds between each row of rings, giving the shade a bubbled look when lowered.

Cloud shade is cut two to three times the width of the window, then shirred across the upper edge to create a soft heading. The lower edge of the shade falls into gentle poufs.

Balloon shade is also cut two to two-and-one-half times the width of the window, but its fullness is folded into oversized inverted pleats at the heading and lower edge. This shade also has permanent poufs at the bottom.

Insulated shade is a basic Roman shade made with insulated lining and a magnetic edge-seal. These shades block out heat or cold, and help regulate temperature extremes at windows.

Roller shade takes on a custom look when made to coordinate with fabrics in the room. These shades, stiffened with a fusible shade backing, are easy to make because they require very little sewing.

Two Ways to Mount Shades

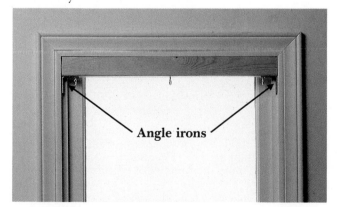

Angle irons

Screws

Inside-mounted shade fits completely inside window opening. Accurate construction and mounting is important. Attach the shade to 1 × 2 mounting board; then attach board to top of window frame with angle irons or screws. Finished width and length of shade are equal to width and length of window opening.

Outside-mounted shade is attached to mounting board, which is secured with screws or angle irons above the window. Finished shade is the same width as the mounting board and covers the frame when lowered. Finished shade length equals distance from top of board to sill or apron. Use this method for windows of different sizes or out-of-square windows.

Roman Shade

Roman shades have a tailored appearance that complements many styles of decor. Use them alone or add cornices, curtains, or draperies.

Like roller shades, Roman shades are flat and smooth when down. When pulled up, they take up more space at the top because they pleat softly instead of rolling. If you want the raised shade to clear the window completely, mount it on the wall above the window. This also adds apparent height to the window. A system of evenly spaced cords and rings on the back of the shade causes the shade to pleat when pulled. A weight bar near the bottom of the shade adds stability and aids smooth tracking.

The choice of fabric affects the look of the finished shade. Sturdy, firm fabrics work best for the pleats of these shades. Lightweight, softer fabrics may be used, but the shades will be less crisp-looking. Roman shades are usually lined. This gives added body to the shade, prevents fabric fading, and gives windows a uniform appearance from the outside.

You may need to seam fabric or lining to create enough width for the shades. Be sure to consider these seams when measuring for construction. Additional fabric may be needed to match a print, plaid, or other design.

To make measuring and construction easier and more accurate, use a folding cardboard cutting board on your work surface.

✂ Cutting Directions

Determine width and length of finished shade. Cut decorator fabric for shade 3" (7.5 cm) wider and 3" (7.5 cm) longer than finished shade.

Cut lining with width equal to finished width of shade; length equal to finished length plus 3" (7.5 cm).

Cut facing strip from lining fabric, 5" (12.5 cm) wide; length equal to finished width of shade plus 2" (5 cm).

YOU WILL NEED

Decorator fabric for shade.

Lining fabric for lining and facing strip.

Mounting board, 1 × 2, cut to size for inside or outside mounting (page 47). Paint ends of board or cover with matching fabric.

Screw eyes or pulleys, large enough to hold all the pull cords. Number should equal the number of columns.

Shade cord for each column of rings. Each cord must be long enough to go up the shade, across the top, and partway down the side for pulling.

Plastic rings, ½" (1.3 cm), equal to number of columns multiplied by number of horizontal rows. Or use ring tape with 6" (15 cm) spaces the length of the shade times the number of columns plus 6" (15 cm) for each column.

Weight rod, one ⅜" (1 cm) brass rod or ½" (1.3 cm) rustproof flat bar, cut ½" (1.3 cm) shorter than finished width of shade.

White glue or liquid fray preventer.

Awning cleat.

Staple gun or tacks.

Drapery pull (optional).

How to Make a Roman Shade

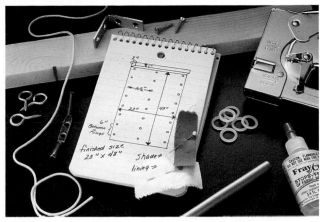

1) **Sketch** the shade to use as a guide for ring locations, page 50, step 7. Cut shade fabric; seam for width, if necessary. If fabric ravels, finish side edges with zigzag stitch or liquid fray preventer.

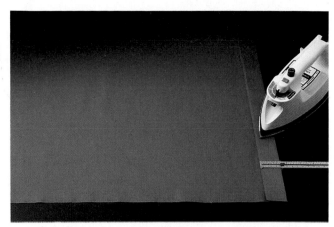

2) **Place** shade fabric wrong side up on work surface. Mark finished width. Press 1½" (3.8 cm) side hems.

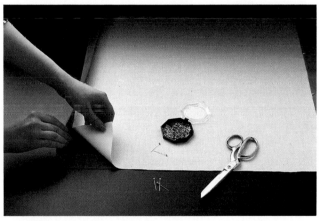

3) **Place** lining on shade fabric, wrong sides together. Slip lining under side hems. Smooth and press lining. Pin in place; slipstitch, if desired.

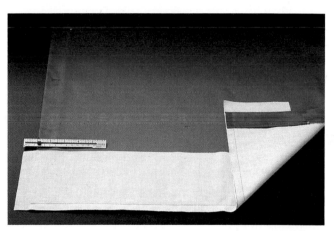

4) **Center** and pin facing strip on right side of shade, even with lower edge, with 1" (2.5 cm) extending at each side. Stitch ½" (1.3 cm) from lower edge. Press toward wrong side of shade.

5) **Fold** and press facing extensions to back of shade so they do not show on the right side. Fuse or stitch in place.

6) **Turn** under raw edge of facing 1½" (3.8 cm); turn under again 3" (7.5 cm). Stitch along folded edge. Stitch again, 1" (2.5 cm) from first stitching to form pocket for weight rod.

(Continued on next page.)

How to Make a Roman Shade (continued)

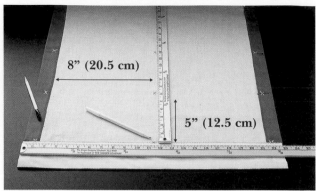

7) Mark locations for rings with rows and columns of X's. First, mark outside columns 1" (2.5 cm) from shade edges so rings hold side hems in place. Space columns 8" to 12" (20.5 to 30.5 cm) apart across shade. Position bottom row just above the rod pocket. Space horizontal rows 5" to 8" (12.5 to 20.5 cm) apart.

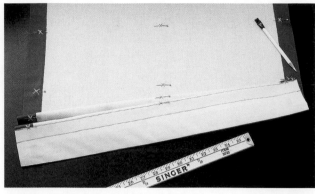

8) Pin through both layers of fabric at center of ring markings, with pins parallel to bottom of shade. Fold shade in accordion pleats at pins to position shade for machine or hand stitching of rings. If using ring tape, omit steps 9a and 9b.

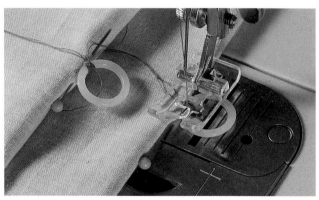

9a) Attach rings by placing fold under presser foot with ring next to fold. Set stitch length at 0 and zigzag at widest setting. Secure ring with 8 to 10 stitches, catching small amount of fold in each stitch. Lock stitches by adjusting needle to penetrate fabric in one place (width setting 0) for 2 or 3 stitches.

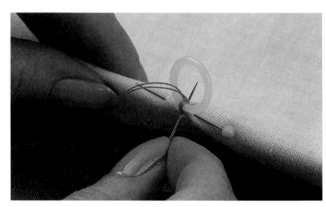

9b) Tack rings by hand if zigzag is not available. Use double thread. Secure with 4 or 5 stitches in one place, through both fabric layers. Reinforce all rings in bottom row with extra stitches; they hold the weight of the fabric.

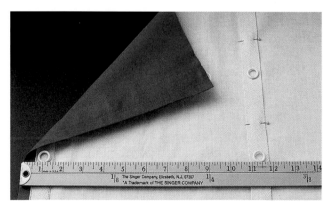

9c) Use ring tape instead of rings, if desired. Turn under ½" (1.3 cm) at bottom of tape and place at top of rod pocket. Pin tape to shade in columns, lining up rings horizontally. Stitch both long edges and bottom of tape with zipper foot, stitching all tapes in same direction.

10) Staple and tack shade to top of mounting board. If shade is mounted outside window frame, paint or wrap the board with lining fabric before attaching shade. This gives the shade a finished look.

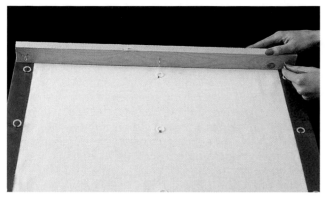

11) Insert screw eyes on mounting board to line up with columns; place one screw eye above each column. On heavy or wide shades, use pulley instead of screw eyes.

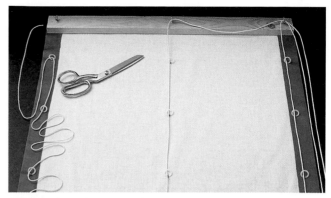

12) Cut lengths of cord, one for each column of rings. Each cord will be a different length; cords go up the shade, across the top and partway down one side. String cord through rings and screw eyes, with excess cord on one side for pulling.

13) Tie a nonslip knot in bottom ring. Apply white glue to knot and ends of cord to prevent knot from slipping.

14) File ends of weight rod or cover ends with tape. Insert rod into rod pocket and slipstitch end closed. A galvanized or iron rod, painted to resist rusting, can be used instead of a brass rod.

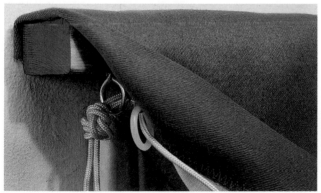

15) Mount shade (page 47). Adjust cords with shade lowered so the tension on all cords is equal. Tie cords in a knot just below screw eye. Braid cords and secure at bottom with a knot or drapery pull.

16) Center awning cleat on edge of window frame or on wall. Wind cord around cleat to secure shade position when the shade is raised.

Stitched-tuck Shade

Narrow stitched tucks along each fold line add interest to this tailored version of the Roman shade. Read about Roman shades on pages 48 to 51 before beginning this project.

To determine the number of tucks, subtract 3" (7.5 cm) for the hem from finished length of shade. Divide this number by 3" (7.5 cm), the approximate spacing between tucks, to get the number of tucks. Round this figure to the nearest whole number. To determine the spacing between tucks, divide the finished length of shade by the number of tucks (as determined above). Rings will be placed on alternate tucks, beginning with the bottom tuck.

✂ Cutting Directions

Cut decorator fabric and lining as for Roman shade (page 48), adding ½" (1.3 cm) for each tuck to the length of both fabrics. Also cut facing strip from lining fabric, 5" (12.5 cm.) wide; length equal to finished shade width plus 2" (5 cm).

YOU WILL NEED

Decorator fabric for shade.

Lining fabric for lining and facing strip.

Notions: mounting board, plastic rings, screw eyes or pulleys, shade cord, weight rod, white glue, awning cleat, and staple gun, as for Roman shade.

How to Make a Stitched-tuck Shade

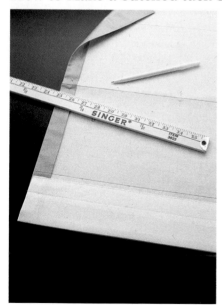

1) Follow directions for Roman shade, pages 49 and 50, steps 1 to 7, except space horizontal rows as figured above. Draw horizontal lines across wrong side of shade at ring locations. Baste lining and outer fabric together on each line.

2) Remove water-soluble pen markings. Fold and press sharp crease exactly on each basting line, right sides together. Bring opposite folds together, accordion-pleat style, and press crease in each fold. Machine-baste as in step 1.

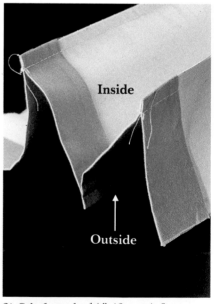

Inside

Outside

3) Stitch tucks ¼" (6 mm) from creased edges on right side and wrong side of shade. Remove basting. Complete the shade following the directions for a Roman shade, pages 50 and 51, steps 9a to 16. Do not use ring tape.

Hobbled Shade

The hobbled shade falls into soft folds, held in place by twill tape. Read about Roman shades (pages 48 to 51) before beginning this project.

To determine the number of folds, double the finished length of the shade and subtract 3" (7.5 cm); then divide this number by 7" (18 cm), the approximate spacing between the folds. Round this figure to the nearest whole number. To determine the actual spacing between the folds, divide twice the finished length of the shade minus 3" (7.5 cm) by the number of folds.

✂ Cutting Directions

Cut decorator fabric and lining as for Roman shade (page 48), doubling the length for both fabrics. Cut facing strip from lining fabric, 5" (12.5 cm) wide; length of facing strip is equal to finished shade width plus 2" (5 cm). Cut twill tape for each column, with length equal to finished length of shade plus 3" (7.5 cm).

YOU WILL NEED

Decorator fabric for shade.

Lining fabric for lining and facing strip.

Twill tape, ½" (1.3 cm) wide.

Notions: mounting board, plastic rings, screw eyes or pulleys, shade cord, weight rod, white glue, awning cleat, and staple gun, as for Roman shade.

How to Make a Hobbled Shade

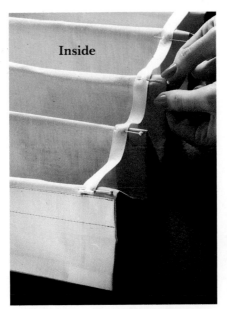

1) Follow steps 1 to 7 on pages 49 and 50, except space horizontal rows on shade as figured above for actual spacing between folds. Mark tapes at intervals halfway between rings on shade, beginning at top of rod pocket.

2) Pin tapes to the shade, lining up marks on tapes with marks on shade. The excess fabric between the markings forms folds on the right side of the shade.

3) Tack the rings in place, catching the tape and both layers of the fabric at each ring. Complete shade following directions for Roman shade, pages 50 and 51, steps 10 to 16.

Cloud Shade

The cloud shade is another easy-to-make variation of the Roman shade with a softly gathered heading. Because this shade has a light, airy look, lining is usually not necessary. Lightweight, soft fabrics are suggested for cloud shades.

A cloud shade can be mounted inside or outside the window frame. Because of the gathered heading and billowy appearance, it is usually used alone.

The heading on this cloud shade is neatly gathered, using a self-styling tape with a "fuzzy" loop face that clings to hook tape attached to the mounting board. You can select from several styles of sew-in or fusible tape, including pencil-pleat tape, multi-cord shirring tape, or smocking tape. The tape style you select determines the amount of fullness required; most require two to two-and-one-half times fullness.

Cloud shades may be mounted on a curtain rod or wooden pole. In this case, allow extra length for sewing the rod pocket and heading (page 31) and insert screw eyes directly into the window frame or into a mounting board installed separately.

Read about Roman shades on pages 48 to 51 before beginning this project.

✂ Cutting Directions

Determine the finished width of the shade including returns if using an outside mount. Cut the fabric with the width equal to two to three times the finished width plus 4" (10 cm) for side hems. Exact fullness needed is determined by the styling tape. Seam fabric widths together as necessary for the cut width. The cut length is equal to the finished length plus 15" (38 cm) for the turn-under at the upper edge, the lower hem, and the lower pouf.

Cut a strip of fabric for covering the weight rod, 1" (2.5 cm) longer than the finished width of the shade and 1" (2.5 cm) wider that the rod circumference.

YOU WILL NEED

Decorator fabric for shade and weight rod cover.

Self-styling tape, sew-in or fusible, with loop face.

Hook tape.

Notions: mounting board, plastic rings, screw eyes, shade cord, weight rod, white glue, awning cleat, and staple gun, as for Roman shade.

How to Make a Cloud Shade

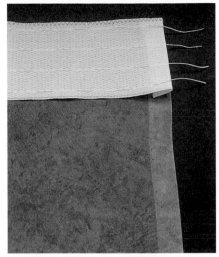

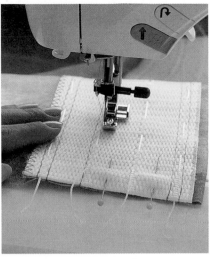

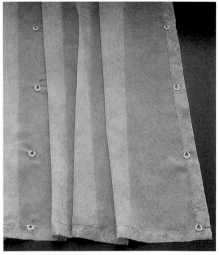

1) Seam fabric as necessary for width, using French seams (page 19). Press under and stitch 1" (2.5 cm) double-fold side hems. Press under and stitch 1" (2.5 cm) double-fold hem pocket at lower edge. Cut styling tape to width of hemmed panel plus 2" (5 cm). Turn under 1" (2.5 cm) on tape ends, keeping cords free. Place tape right side up on right side of panel, aligning lower edge of tape to upper edge of panel. Overcast edges together.

2) Fold tape and panel to wrong side, forming fold ¼" (6 mm) above upper edge of tape; press and pin. Stitch tape to panel, stitching next to cords. Stitch all stitching lines in same direction to avoid ripples.

3) Mark positions for rings. Space horizontal rows about 6" (15 cm) apart. Space vertical columns 18" to 36" (46 to 91.5 cm) apart; columns will be closer after styling tape is gathered. Attach rings, page 50, step 9a or 9b.

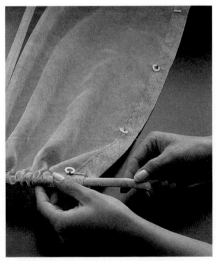

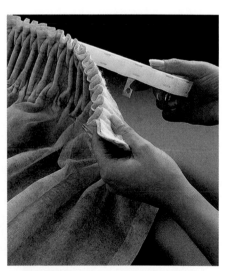

4) Knot all cords together, or knot them in pairs, at each end of tape. At one end, pull evenly on cords to gather fabric, adjusting width of heading to desired finished width. Knot cords in pairs at side of shade. Cut off excess cord length, or conceal cords behind shade. If cords are not cut, shade can be smoothed for laundering.

5) Fold weight rod cover strip in half lengthwise, wrong sides together. Stitch ⅜" (1 cm) seam on one end and the long side; turn right side out. Insert weight rod; stitch end closed. Insert covered rod into hem pocket, distributing fullness of pocket evenly along rod. Slipstitch hem ends closed. Tack hem to rod cover at ends and near each lower ring.

6) Staple hook tape to mounting board. Attach shade to board. Or staple shade to board, hiding staples in folds of heading. Follow steps 11 to 13 on page 51. Tie together bottom three rings of each column. This creates a permanent pouf in the shade, even when it is completely lowered. Mount shade as on page 51, steps 15 and 16.

Balloon Shade

The balloon shade is another variation of the Roman shade. A series of evenly placed box pleats gives this shade controlled fullness when lowered and a billowy, soft effect when raised. This shade is suitable for an inside mount or an outside mount with a shallow projection.

When made from soft, sheer, or unlined fabrics, balloon shades drape into gentle poufs. With tightly woven, mediumweight fabrics, the shades have a crisper, more tailored appearance. Avoid fabrics with heavily glazed finishes which retain wrinkles and creases rather than relax and fall smoothly. Lining is optional. Follow the directions for a lined Roman shade, page 49, step 3, if opaqueness or additional body is required.

Read about Roman shades on pages 48 to 51 before beginning this project.

✂ Cutting Directions

Determine the finished width of the shade. Cut the fabric with the width equal to two to two-and-one-half times the finished width plus 4" (10 cm) for side hems. Seam fabric widths together as necessary, positioning the seam at the inside fold of a pleat. The cut length is equal to the finished length plus 12" (30.5 cm) for the lower pouf plus the projection of the mounting board for mounting. Also cut a facing strip 2" (5 cm) wide and 1" (2.5 cm) longer than the finished width of the shade.

Cut a narrow strip of paper, such as adding machine paper, the same length as the cut width of the shade; make a pattern to help you position the pleats accurately on the shade.

YOU WILL NEED

Fabric for shade and facing strip.

Lining fabric (optional).

Notions: mounting board, plastic rings, screw eyes, shade cord, weight rod, white glue, awning cleat, and staple gun, as for Roman shade.

How to Make a Balloon Shade

1) Mark 2" (5 cm) hem allowance at each side of pattern. Mark pleat foldlines in pattern 9" to 12" (23 to 30.5 cm) apart and about 6" (15 cm) deep. Mark half pleat at each end. Fold pleats, and check for fit. Seam fabric as necessary for width, positioning seam at inside fold of a pleat. Turn under and press 1" (2.5 cm) double-fold side hems; straight-stitch. Place pattern on shade at lower edge. Mark pleat fold lines with ¼" (6 mm) snips. Repeat along upper edge.

2) Fold, pin, and press pleats the entire length of shade. The side hems are entirely hidden under the end pleats. Stitch ½" (1.3 cm) from lower edge to secure pleats. Stitch a distance from upper edge equal to the projection of the mounting board. Finish upper edge using zigzag or serger.

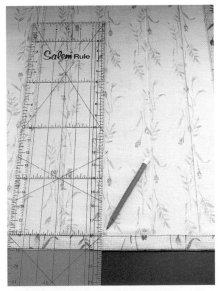

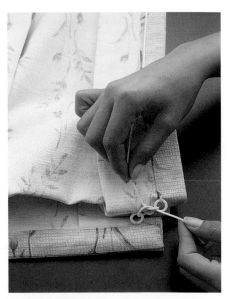

3) Press under ½" (1.3 cm) on short ends and one long side of facing strip. Pin remaining long side to bottom of shade, right sides together. Stitch ½" (1.3 cm) seam. Turn to wrong side of shade; press. Edgestitch along fold, forming weight rod pocket.

4) Mark positions for rings in columns at side hems and at center of each pleat; mark bottom row at upper edge of weight rod pocket, and space rows evenly about 6" (15 cm) apart. Stitch rings to shade through one layer of fabric. Insert weight bar; stitch ends closed.

5) Staple shade to mounting board, with finished upper edge along back of board. String shade as for Roman shades, page 51, steps 12 and 13. Tie together bottom three rings of each column. This creates a permanent pouf in the shade, even when it is completely lowered. Mount shade as on page 51, steps 15 and 16.

Insulated Roman Shade

Insulated Roman shades are practical for sewers who are energy conscious. These shades help your home stay warm in winter and cool in summer; they pay for themselves in reduced heating and cooling costs. Read about Roman shades on pages 48 to 51 before beginning this project.

The shades are lined with insulated lining, the portion of the shade that provides effective insulation when the shade is lowered. Insulated lining consists of four layers (see below), quilted in 8" (20.5 cm) channels, with 4" (10 cm) channels at the edges.

Because the insulating layers are quilted, the time-consuming task of making your own layers is eliminated. Quilting also reduces bulk, making the finished shade more attractive and easier to handle.

The quilting lines mark the horizontal ring positions on the Roman shade. (Channels run on the *lengthwise* grain of the fabric but *crosswise* on the finished shade.) This eliminates much of the measuring normally required to mark ring positions.

Combined with an edge-seal system, insulated shades can reduce heat loss and heat gain from windows even more effectively. An edge-seal system consists of flexible magnetic strips placed along the sides of the window and inside the shade edges. On closed shades, these strips form an airtight seal which keeps warm, moist air from flowing around the edges of the shade, causing energy loss and condensation. The magnetic strips may be painted to match the window frame.

Before making the shade, decide how it will be mounted to determine the length and width of the finished shade. The three types of mounts that may be used for insulated Roman shades are *inside, outside,* and *hybrid*. Descriptions of inside and outside mounts are given on pages 47 and 62.

The hybrid mount (page 62) is especially good for insulated shades. Although the mounting board is cut and mounted like an inside mount, the shade is about ¾" (2 cm) wider on each side and overlaps the window to control airflow around the edges.

✂ Cutting Directions

Cut fabric for shade 3" (7.5 cm) wider and 12" (30.5 cm) longer than finished shade. Cut insulated lining with width equal to finished width of shade; length equal to finished length plus about 4" (10 cm) for mounting.

YOU WILL NEED

Decorator fabric for shade.

Insulated lining, channel quilted.

Magnetic tape for edge-seal system.

Notions: mounting board, plastic rings, screw eyes, pulley or pulley lock, shade cord, weight rod, awning cleat, glue, and staple gun, as for Roman shade.

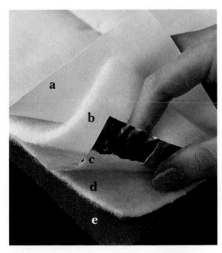

Insulated lining consists of four layers: cotton/polyester lining (**a**); polyester batting (**b**); polyethelene moisture vapor barrier (**c**); heat-reflecting Mylar® (**d**). With the addition of the decorator fabric (**e**), the shade provides five layers of insulation.

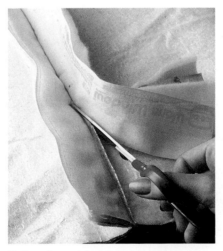

Splice for added length by joining two pieces on quilting lines. This maintains 8" (20.5 cm) between lines. Stitch through all layers, applying slight tension in front of and behind needle. Trim and grade seam to ¼" (6 mm), holding scissors at an angle.

Edge-seal system consists of strips of magnetic tape placed on the window frame to correspond to strips of tape placed inside the shade. When pressed together, magnetic strips form a seal that shuts out hot or cold air. To release seal, pull shade out at lower edge.

How to Sew an Insulated Roman Shade

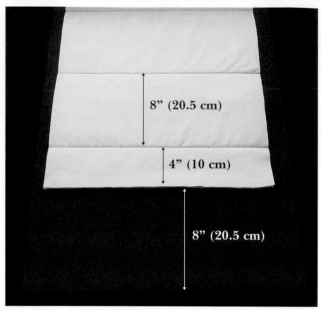

8" (20.5 cm)

4" (10 cm)

8" (20.5 cm)

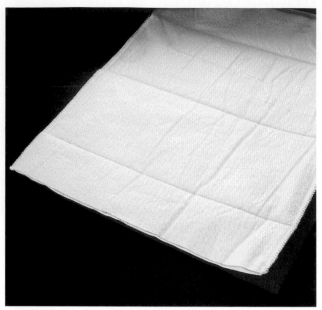

1) Cut insulated lining and shade fabric as directed in cutting directions (page 59). Splice lining for added length, if necessary, as directed on page 59. Position 4" (10 cm) channel to lower edge of the shade, 8" (20.5) from cut edge.

2) Pin shade and insulated lining, with right sides together and top and side edges even. The shade fabric will not lie flat because of the 3" (7.5 cm) added for side hems. Stitch ½" (1.3 cm) seams. Zigzag or edgestitch close to cut edge to reduce bulk and prevent insulation from curling.

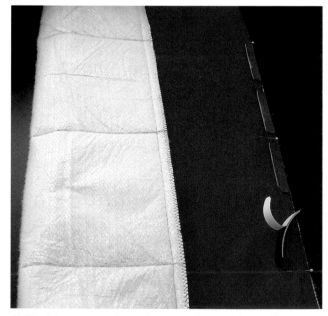

3) Place the roll of magnetic tape on newspaper and spray-paint one edge of the roll. This marks the lengthwise polarity. The polarity is important when attaching tape to shade and window. Separate scored lengths of tape or cut 3¼" (8.2 cm) lengths. Round tape corners with scissors to prevent sharp corners from tearing fabric.

4) Position two strips of magnetic tape in each channel, placing strips on the seam allowance on wrong side of shade fabric. Place all strips in the same direction, using painted edges as guide to polarity. Peel off paper backing and press firmly. Do not place magnetic tape in mounting area at top of shade or in lower hem area.

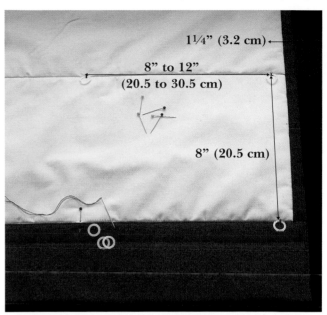

5) Place a 2½" (6.5 cm) strip of magnetic tape on the right side of shade fabric on the seam allowance of lower hem area, just below edge of insulation. If magnetic seal is used on lower edge, firmly press long strip of magnetic tape across shade at lower edge of insulation.

6) Turn shade right side out. Turn under 4" (10 cm) double-fold hem at lower edge. Be sure lower edge is square. Taper side hem edges slightly so they do not show on right side. Stitch close to hem fold; stitch 1" (2.5 cm) from first stitching line to form rod pocket. Mark positions for rings on quilting rows. Place rings 1¼" (3.2 cm) from sides. Space columns 8" to 12" (20.5 to 30.5 cm) apart. Pin through all layers at each mark to prevent shifting. Tack on rings.

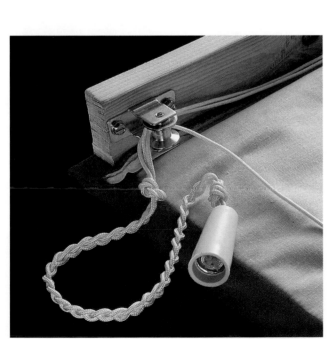

7) Wrap ends of weight rod with tape, or file rough edges to reduce wear on shade fabric. Insert weight into rod pocket. Slipstitch opening closed. Attach a plain or lock pulley for first column on the pull side of shade. Pulley supports the additional weight and accommodates more strings than screw eyes do. Attach weighted shade pull. Mount and string shade (page 62).

8) Clean window frame with alcohol to ensure a tight bond. Place long strips of magnetic tape on the sides of the shade to match polarity; mark the top of the strip. Remove strip from shade; peel off backing, and press strip to the window frame.

How to Mount an Insulated Shade Using an Outside Mount

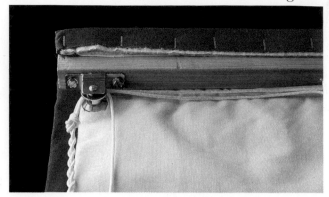

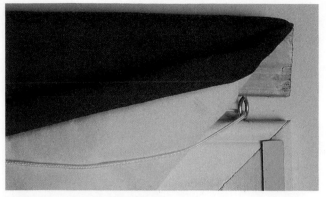

1) Cut 1 × 2 board to the width of finished shade. Wrap shade up and over edge of board; staple to back. Place pulley and screw eyes directly above columns of rings.

2) String as for Roman shade, page 51, steps 12 and 13. Screw mounting board into wall. Attach awning cleat to side of window frame or wall if not using a lock pulley.

How to Mount an Insulated Shade Using an Inside Mount

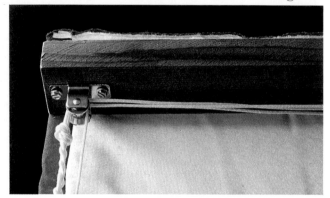

1) Cut 1 × 2 board to fit inside window opening. Wrap shade over edge of board; staple. Place pulley and screw eyes directly above columns of rings. String as for Roman shade, page 51, steps 12 and 13.

2) Screw mounting board into top of window frame. Attach awning cleat to side of window frame or wall if not using a lock pulley.

How to Mount an Insulated Shade Using a Hybrid Mount

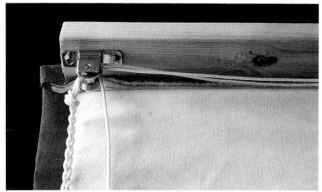

1) Cut 1 × 2 board to fit inside window opening. Fold shade over at upper edge to finished length. Place fold along upper edge of board so sides of shade extend equally beyond board. Lift shade and staple to mounting board near the fold.

2) Place narrow cardboard strip over stapled portion of shade with upper edge of cardboard even with upper edge of mounting board; staple. String as for Roman shade, page 51, steps 12 and 13. Screw mounting board onto top of window frame. Attach awning cleat to side of window frame or wall.

Roller Shade

Mount roller shades inside the window opening with ¼" (6 mm) or less clearance around the edges to increase the energy efficiency of a window. Roller shades can also be hung on brackets on the frame or wall outside the window. For inside mounting, measure from outside edges of brackets. If you do not want the roller to show, use reverse brackets, and cut the roller to fit.

Select a firmly woven fabric that bonds well. Water-resistant and stain-resistant fabrics that are treated with silicone do not bond.

✂ Cutting Directions

Cut fabric 1" to 2" (2.5 to 5 cm) wider than jamb or bracket measurement, and 12" (30.5 cm) longer than area to be covered top to bottom. Cut fusible backing with same dimensions.

YOU WILL NEED

Fabric and fusible shade backing for shade.

Wooden slat, ¼" (6 mm) shorter than finished width of shade.

Roller to fit window width.

Staple gun with ¼" (6 mm) staples, masking tape or other strong tape, and white glue.

Shade pull (optional).

How to Make a Roller Shade

1) Mark center at upper and lower edges of fabric and fusible backing. Place the wrong side of the fabric to the fusible side of the backing, matching edges and center markings.

2) Fuse according to manufacturer's directions for time and temperature, working from center to outside and from top to bottom. Allow shade to cool before moving so bond is permanently set.

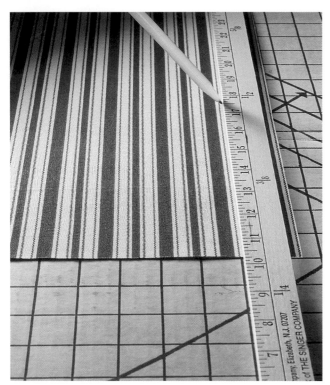

3) Use a yardstick to mark cutting lines on sides of shade; distance between cutting lines should be equal to finished width of shade. Use a carpenter's square or cutting board for right angles.

4) Cut carefully along cutting lines with smooth, even strokes. To keep edges from raveling, put a small amount of white glue on your finger and draw it along each edge. Let dry completely.

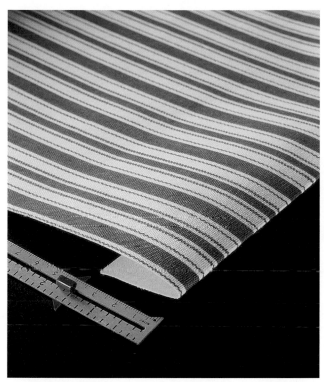

5) Fold under 1½" (3.8 cm) along lower edge for a straight hem and slat pocket. Use carpenter's square to check right angles at corners.

6) Stitch 1¼" (3.2 cm) from folded edge, using long stitches to form a pocket for the slat. Press pocket. Insert the slat. Attach shade pull, if desired.

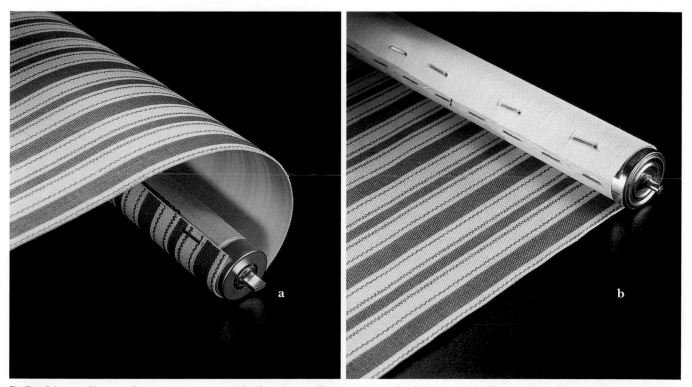

7) Position roller under or over top of shade, depending on how shade is to roll. To attach roller under shade, place flat pin to the right **(a);** to attach roller over shade, place round pin to the right **(b).** Make sure wrong side of hem is turned so it will not show when shade is hung. Staple or tape shade to roller.

Pillows

1

2

3

4

5

6

7

8

9

10

Pillow Fashions

Pillow styles range from simple to elaborate. Choice of technique affects your sewing time. Choose a simple knife-edge pillow, or invest more time in tailoring a box pillow complete with welting and a zipper.

1) Neckrolls are small, round bolsters that are often trimmed with lace or ruffles. They are made with a drawstring closure at each end of a tube.

2) Shirred welted pillow is made by inserting gathered welting in the seam around the pillow. Welting is gathered using a technique known as shirring to gather the fabric strip that covers the cord. Make welting in matching or contrasting fabric to add a decorative finish to a pillow.

3) Shirred box pillow uses shirring to gather both edges of the boxing strip. This makes the pillow softer than the traditional box pillow.

4) Flange pillow has a single or double, flat self-border, usually 2" (5 cm) wide, around a plump knife-edge pillow.

5) Mock box pillow is a variation of the knife-edge pillow, with shaped corners to add depth. Corners made using *gathered* style are tied inside the pillow.

6) Ruffled pillow features gathered lace or ruffles made in single or double layers. Pillow tops framed by ruffles in matching or contrasting fabric make attractive showcases for needlepoint, quilting, or embroidery.

7) Box pillow has the added depth of a straight or shirred boxing strip. It can be soft for a scatter pillow or firm for a chair cushion or floor pillow.

8) Mock box pillow can be made with *mitered* corners to create a tailored box shape.

9) Knife-edge pillow is the easiest pillow to make. It consists of two pieces of fabric sewn together, turned right side out, and stuffed.

10) Welted pillow is a knife-edge pillow with matching or contrasting welting sewn in the seams. Use purchased welting or make your own. Or finish the pillow with a mock welted edge for a welted look without extra sewing time or fabric.

Fabrics, Forms & Fillings

To choose the right fabric for your pillow, consider how the pillow will be used and where it will be placed in your home. For a pillow that will receive hard wear, select a sturdy, firmly woven fabric that will retain its shape.

Pillows get their shape from forms or loose fillings. Loose fillings may be stuffed directly into the pillow covering or encased in a separate liner for easy removal. For ease in laundering or drycleaning, make a separate inner covering or liner for the stuffing, using lightweight muslin or lining fabric, or use purchased pillow forms. Make the liner as you would a knife-edge pillow (pages 70 and 71). Choose from several kinds of forms and fillings.

1) Standard polyester forms are square, round, and rectangular for knife-edge pillows in sizes from 10" to 30" (25.5 to 76 cm). These forms are nonallergenic, washable, do not bunch, and may have muslin or polyester outer coverings.

2) Polyurethane foam is available in sheets ½" to 5" (1.3 to 12.5 cm) thick for firm pillows and cushions. Some stores carry a high-density foam, 4" (10 cm) thick, for extra firm cushions. A salesperson can usually cut a piece to the size of your pillow. If you must cut your own foam, use an electric or serrated knife with silicone lubricant sprayed on the blade.

3) Polyester fiberfill is washable, nonallergenic filling for pillows or pillow liners. Fiberfill comes in loose-pack bags.

4) Polyester upholstery batting can be used for pillows or cushions. For a smooth pillow, sew an inner liner of batting, then stuff with loose fiberfill. Soften the hard edges of polyurethane foam by wrapping the form with batting.

5) Compressed polyester in thicknesses from 1" to 4" (2.5 to 10 cm) is available in precut squares or slabs for use in making cushions. It is washable, nonallergenic, and mildew resistant, making it especially useful for outdoor cushions.

6) Down is washed, quill-less feathers from the breasts of geese and ducks. Down forms make luxurious pillows, though more expensive.

Knife-edge
Pillow or Liner

Knife-edge pillows are plump in the center and flat around the edges. These simple pillows can be made in half an hour.

Use the knife-edge pillow directions to make removable pillow liners. Sew liners from muslin, sheeting, cotton sateen, or similar fabrics.

✂ Cutting Directions

Cut front and back 1" (2.5 cm) larger than finished pillow or liner. For centered zipper closure, add 1" (2.5 cm) to back width; for overlap closure, add 5½" (14 cm).

YOU WILL NEED

Decorator fabric for pillow front and back.

Lining fabric for pillow liner front and back.

Pillow form or polyester fiberfill. Use 8 to 12 oz. (227 to 340 g) fiberfill for a 14" (35.5 cm) pillow, depending on desired firmness.

Zipper or other closure (optional) may be inserted (pages 86 to 88).

How to Make a Knife-edge Pillow or Liner

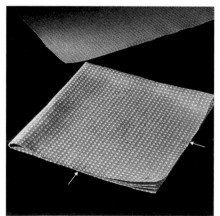

1) Fold front into fourths. Mark a point halfway between the corner and the fold on each open side. At corner, mark a point ½" (1.3 cm) from each raw edge.

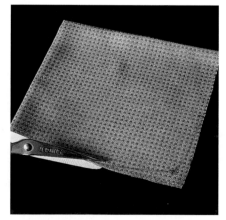

2) Trim from center mark to corner, gradually tapering from the edge to the ½" (1.3 cm) mark. Taper from ½" (1.3 cm) mark to center mark on opposite edge.

3) Unfold front and use it as a pattern for trimming back so that all corners are slightly rounded. This will eliminate dog-ears on the corners of the finished pillow.

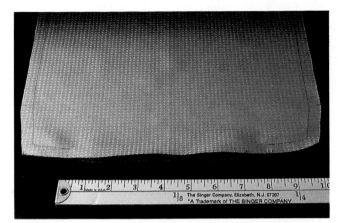

4) Pin front to back, right sides together. Stitch ½" (1.3 cm) seam, leaving opening on one side for turning and stuffing. Backstitch at the beginning and end of seam.

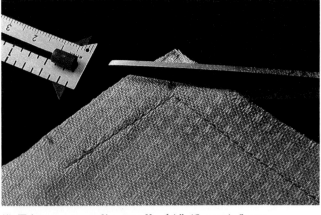

5) Trim corners diagonally, ⅛" (3 mm) from stitching. On pillows with curved edges or round corners, clip seam allowance to stitching at intervals along curves.

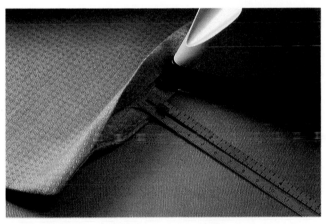

6) Turn pillow right side out, pulling out corners. Press the seams. Press under the seam allowances in the opening.

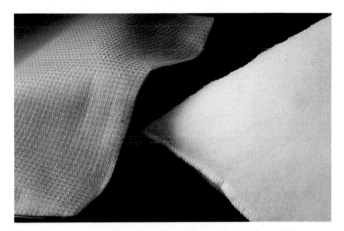

7a) Insert a purchased pillow form into the pillow, or stuff the pillow with polyester fiberfill as in step 7b, below. Use a removable form or liner in pillows that will be drycleaned or laundered.

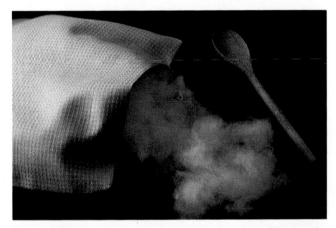

7b) Stuff pillow or liner with polyester fiberfill, gently pulling pieces apart to fluff and separate fibers. Work filling into corners, using long, blunt tool such as a spoon handle.

8) Pin opening closed and edgestitch close to folded edge, backstitching at beginning and end of the stitching. Or slipstitch opening closed.

Welted Knife-edge Pillow

Welting adds stability to pillows and gives them a more tailored look. Welting is made by covering cord with bias strips.

✂ Cutting Directions

Cut pillow front and back 1" (2.5 cm) larger than finished pillow. For centered zipper closure, add 1" (2.5 cm) to back width; for overlap closure, add 5½" (14 cm). Cut bias strips for welting as in step 1, below.

YOU WILL NEED

Decorator fabric for pillow front, back, and welting.

Cord for welting, 3" (7.5 cm) longer than distance around pillow.

Pillow form or knife-edge liner.

Zipper or other closure (optional) may be inserted (pages 86 to 88).

How to Make a Welted Knife-edge Pillow

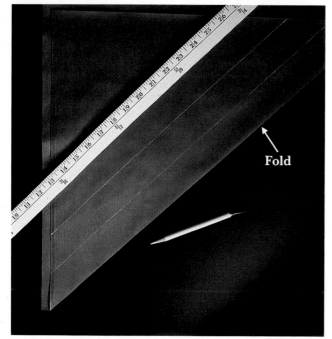

1) Cut bias strips. Determine bias grainline by folding fabric diagonally so selvage aligns with crosswise cut. Mark and cut strips parallel to bias grainline. Cut strips 1" (2.5 cm) wider than cord circumference.

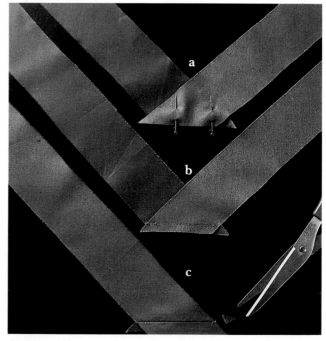

2) Pin strips at right angles, right sides together, offset slightly **(a).** Stitch ¼" (6 mm) seams **(b),** and press open, making one continuous strip equal in length to perimeter of pillow plus 3" (7.5 cm). Trim seam allowances even with edges **(c).**

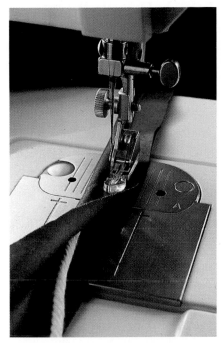

3) Center cord on wrong side of bias strips. Fold strip over cord, aligning raw edges. Using zipper foot on right side of needle, stitch close to cord.

4) Pin the welting to the right side of the pillow front, with raw edges aligned. To ease corners, clip seam allowances to stitching at corners.

5) Stitch, crowding the cord; stop stitching 2" (5 cm) from the point where ends of welting will meet. Leave needle in fabric. Cut off one end of welting so it overlaps the other end by 1" (2.5 cm).

6) Take out 1" (2.5 cm) of stitching from each end of welting. Trim cord ends so they just meet.

7) Fold under ½" (1.3 cm) of overlapping bias strip. Lap it around the other end and finish stitching. Pin pillow front to back, right sides together.

8) Stitch inside stitching line, using zipper foot; crowd stitching against cord. Leave opening. Finish as for knife-edge pillow, page 71, steps 5 to 7b. Slipstitch opening closed.

Mock Box Pillow

Mock box pillows are variations of knife-edge pillows and can be made in three styles. Corners on gathered styles are tied inside the pillow. Mitered styles have a short seam across each corner to create a tailored box shape. Pleated styles have neat tucks at each corner. Pillows with gathers or pleats are sometimes called Turkish pillows.

✂ Cutting Directions

Cut pillow front and back the size of the pillow form plus 1" (2.5 cm) for seams. For centered zipper closure, add 1" (2.5 cm) to back width; for overlap closure, add 5½" (14 cm).

YOU WILL NEED

Knife-edge pillow form. Or make a mock box pillow liner using the directions below.

Decorator fabric for pillow front and back.

Zipper or other closure (optional) may be inserted in center back or side seams (page 88).

How to Make a Mock Box Pillow with Mitered Corners

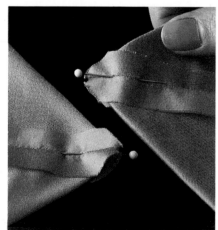

1) Stitch as directed on page 71, step 4. Press seams open. Separate front and back at corners. Center seams on each side of corner, on top of each other. Pin through seam.

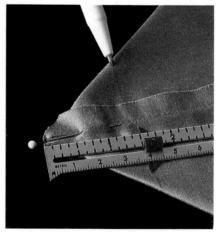

2) Measure on side seam from corner to half the finished depth; for example, for pillow 3" (7.5 cm) deep, measure 1½" (3.8 cm) from corner. Draw a line perpendicular to the seam.

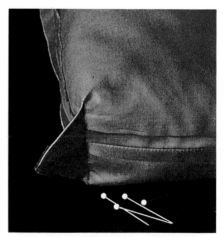

3) Stitch across corner of pillow on marked line; backstitch at beginning and end. Do not trim seam. Finish pillow as for knife-edge pillow, page 71, steps 6 to 7b. Slipstitch opening closed.

How to Make a Mock Box Pillow with Gathered Corners

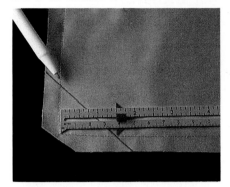

1) Stitch pillow front to pillow back as for knife-edge pillow, page 71, steps 4 and 5. Measure on each seamline from corner to finished pillow depth. Draw diagonal line across the corner.

2) Hand-baste on diagonal line with topstitching and buttonhole twist or doubled thread. Pull up thread to gather.

3) Wrap thread several times around corner; secure with knot. Do not trim corner. Repeat for each corner. Finish as for knife-edge pillow, page 71, steps 6 to 7b. Slipstitch opening closed.

How to Make a Mock Box Pillow with Pleated Corners

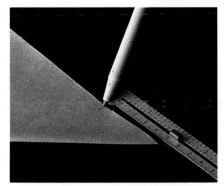

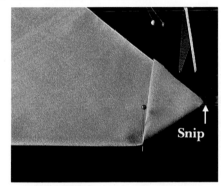

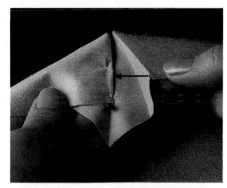

1) Fold corner in half diagonally. On raw edge, measure from the corner to half the finished pillow depth plus ½" (1.3 cm); for example, for pillow 3" (7.5 cm) deep, measure 2" (5 cm) from the corner.

2) Mark measured point with ¼" (6 mm) snips through both seam allowances. Fold corner back at snips to form triangle. Mark fold with pin. Press triangle in place.

3) Spread corner flat, right side up. Fold fabric from snip to pin; bring fold to pressed center mark, forming pleat. Pin pleat in place. Repeat for other side.

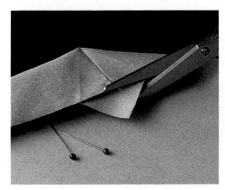

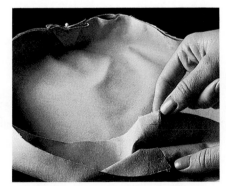

4) Baste across pleat, ½" (1.3 cm) from raw edge, removing pins as you stitch. Trim triangle-shaped piece from corner. Repeat for each corner of front and back.

5) Pin front to back, right sides together, with front tucked into back to form a "basket." Match pleated corners precisely.

6) Stitch ½" (1.3 cm) seam, leaving opening on one side. Finish as for knife-edge pillow, page 71, steps 6 to 7b. Slipstitch opening closed.

Mock Welted Pillow

Mock welted pillows are welted after the pillow is assembled.

✂ Cutting Directions

Cut pillow front 1" (2.5 cm) larger than the finished pillow. Cut back the same length as front. For centered zipper closure, add 1" (2.5 cm) to back width; for overlap closure, add 5½" (14 cm).

YOU WILL NEED

Decorator fabric for pillow front and back.

Zipper, 2" (5 cm) shorter than length of pillow.

Cord, ½" to 1" (1.3 to 2.5 cm), equal in length to distance around the pillow.

Pillow form or knife-edge liner.

How to Make a Mock Welted Pillow

1) Insert zipper closure in center of pillow back, page 88. Trim corners of front and back into curves. Pin front to back, right sides together. Stitch ¼" (6 mm) seam around entire pillow. Turn pillow right side out.

2) Pin cord inside pillow, as tightly as possible against seam. Ends of cord should just meet.

3) Stitch from right side, crowding stitching against cord, using zipper foot. Leave 3" (7.5 cm) opening where cord ends meet.

4) Pull out cord about 4" (10 cm) at each end to gather. Adjust gathers. Cut cord so ends just meet. Tack ends together. Topstitch opening closed, using zipper foot. Insert pillow form or liner.

Box Pillow

Box pillows can be used for cushions as well as for casual pillows. They are firm because of the boxing strip that is sewn between the pillow front and back.

✂ Cutting Directions

Cut pillow front and back 1" (2.5 cm) larger than finished pillow. Cut the boxing strip with length equal to distance around pillow plus 1" (2.5 cm) for seams, width equal to depth of pillow plus 1" (2.5 cm).

YOU WILL NEED

Decorator fabric for pillow front, back, and boxing strip.

Polyurethane foam wrapped in batting. Or make a box pillow liner, using directions below.

How to Make a Box Pillow

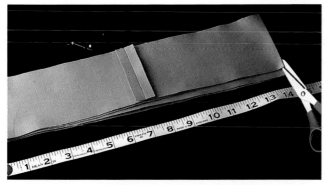

1) Stitch short ends of boxing strip, right sides together, to form continuous loop. Fold loop into fourths and mark each fold with ⅜" (1 cm) clip on both edges.

2) Make and apply welting, if desired, to pillow front and back as on pages 72 and 73, steps 1 to 7. Pin boxing strip to pillow front, right sides together, raw edges even, matching clipped points on strip to pillow corners.

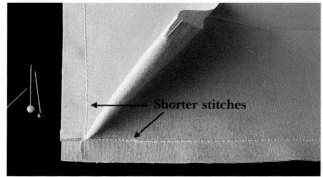

3) Stitch ½" (1.3 cm) seam, shortening stitches for 1" (2.5 cm) on each side of corner; take one or two stitches diagonally across each corner instead of sharp pivot. Use zipper foot if making a welted pillow.

Shorter stitches

4) Pin boxing strip to pillow back, right sides together; match clips to corners. Stitch seam as in step 3, leaving one side open. Press seams, turning under seam allowances at opening. Insert form or liner; slipstitch opening closed.

Ruffled Pillow

Ruffles add interest to a pillow or enhance needlework pillows. Make ruffles from matching or contrasting fabric, or purchase lace or eyelet ruffling.

✂ Cutting Directions

Cut pillow front and back 1" (2.5 cm) larger than finished pillow. Cut ruffle strips twice the desired width plus 1" (2.5 cm) for seam, length two to three times the distance around pillow. Ruffles are usually about 3" (7.5 cm) wide.

YOU WILL NEED

Decorator fabric for pillow front and back and double ruffle.

Purchased ruffling (optional), equal in length to distance around pillow plus 1" (2.5 cm).

Cord, (string, crochet cotton, or dental floss) for gathering.

Pillow form or knife-edge liner.

How to Make a Ruffled Pillow

1) Stitch short ends of ruffle strip with ½" (1.3 cm) seam, right sides together, to form a loop. Fold strip in half lengthwise, wrong sides together; fold into fourths. Mark each fold with a ⅜" (1 cm) clip.

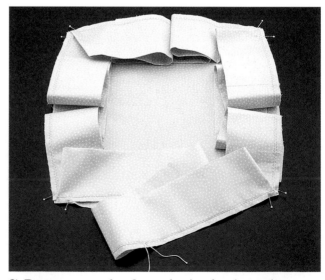

2) Prepare raw edge for gathering by zigzagging over a cord (page 35). For square pillows, match clips on ruffles to corners of pillow front, right sides together and raw edges even; for rectangular pillow, match clips to center of sides, right sides together and raw edges even. Pin.

3) Pull up the gathering cord until ruffle fits each side of the pillow front. Distribute gathers, allowing extra fullness at corners so ruffle will lie flat in finished pillow. Pin ruffle in place.

4) Machine-baste ruffle to pillow front, stitching just inside gathering row.

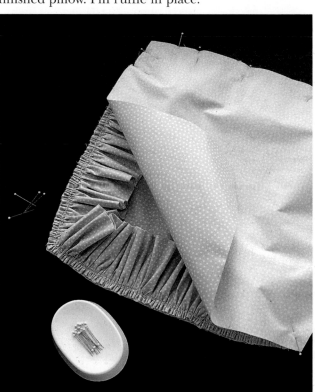

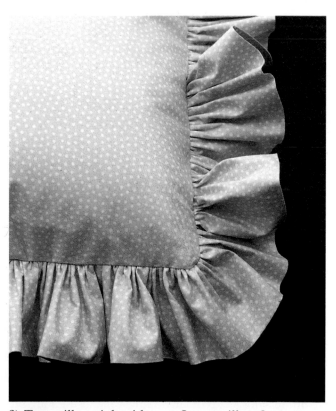

5) Pin pillow back to front, right sides together, with ruffle between pieces. Stitch ½" (1.3 cm) seam, leaving 8" (20.5 cm) opening on one side for turning.

6) Turn pillow right side out. Insert pillow form or knife-edge liner; slipstitch opening closed.

Flange Pillows

A *flange* is a flat border around a plump knife-edge pillow. Flanges may be single or double, and are usually about 2" (5 cm) wide. The double-flange pillow is made with a closure; the single-flange pillow is sewn closed.

✂ Cutting Directions

For single flange, cut pillow front and back 5" (12.5 cm) larger than stuffed inner area. This allows for 2" (5 cm) flange and ½" (1.3 cm) seam on each side.

For double flange, cut pillow front 9" (23 cm) larger than pillow form. This allows for a 2" (5 cm) flange and ½" (1.3 cm) seam on each side. For centered zipper closure, add 1" (2.5 cm) to back width; for overlap closure, add 5½" (14 cm).

YOU WILL NEED

Decorator fabric for pillow front and back.

Polyester fiberfill for single flange pillow, about 6 oz. (170 g) for 12" (30.5 cm) pillow.

Pillow form or knife-edge liner for double flange pillow, to fit inner area.

Zipper for double flange pillow, 2" (5 cm) shorter than length of stuffed inner area (page 88).

How to Make a Single-Flange Pillow

1) Pin pillow front to back, right sides together. Stitch ½" (1.3 cm) seam, leaving 8" (20.5 cm) opening. Turn right side out. Press. Topstitch 2" (5 cm) from edge, beginning and ending at opening.

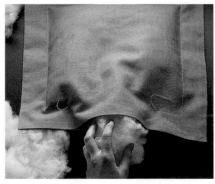

2) Stuff inner area with polyester fiberfill. Work filling into corners, using long blunt tool such as wooden spoon handle. Do not stuff the flange.

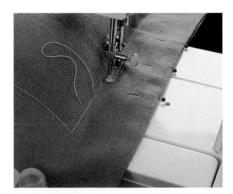

3) Topstitch inner area closed, using zipper foot, starting and ending at first stitching line. Slipstitch flange opening, or edgestitch around entire pillow.

How to Make a Double-Flange Pillow with Mitered Corners

1) Insert zipper (page 88) in pillow back.

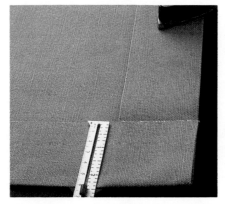

2) Press under 2½" (6.5 cm) on each side of front and back. Place front and back together to make sure corners match; adjust pressed folds if necessary.

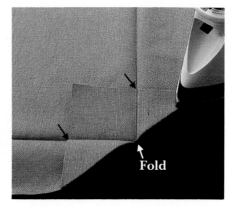

3) Open out corner. Fold corner diagonally so pressed folds match (arrows). Press diagonal fold.

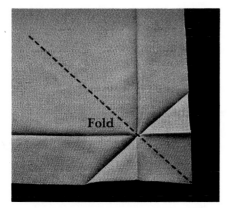

4) Open out corner. Fold through center of corner (dotted line), right sides together.

5) Pin on diagonal fold line, raw edges even. Stitch on fold line at right angle to corner fold.

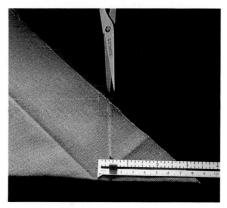

6) Trim seam to ⅜" (1 cm). Press seam open.

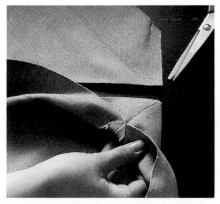

7) Turn corner right side out. Use point turner to get a sharp point. Press edges. Repeat with other corners, front and back.

8) Pin pillow front to back, wrong sides together, matching mitered corners carefully.

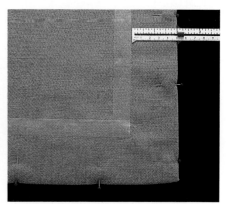

9) Measure 2" (5 cm) from edge for flange; mark stitching line with transparent tape. Topstitch through all thicknesses along edge of tape. Insert pillow form or liner.

Shirred Pillows

Shirred welting or boxing strips give pillows a formal look.

✂ Cutting Directions

For shirred box pillow, cut pillow front and back 1" (2.5 cm) smaller than the pillow form. Cut boxing strip 3½" (9 cm) wide and two to three times longer than distance around form.

For shirred welted pillow, cut pillow front and back 1" (2.5 cm) larger than finished pillow. For welting, cut fabric strips on the bias or crosswise grain, wide enough to cover cord plus 1" (2.5 cm) for seam. The combined length of the strips should be two to three times the distance around pillow.

YOU WILL NEED

Decorator fabric for pillow front and back and for welting or boxing strips.

Cord (if making shirred welting). Cut 3" (7.5 cm) longer than distance around pillow.

Gathering cord (string, crochet cotton, or dental floss).

Pillow form or liner.

How to Make Shirred Welting

1) Join ends of bias strips; press seams open. Stitch one end of cord to wrong side of strip, ⅜" (1 cm) from end of strip. Fold strip around cord, wrong sides together, matching raw edges. Using zipper foot, machine-baste for 6" (15 cm), close to but not crowding cord. Stop stitching with needle in fabric.

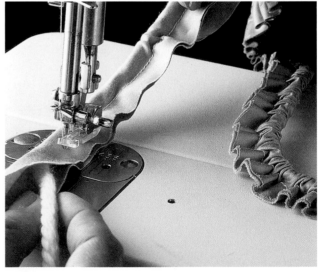

2) Raise presser foot. While gently pulling cord, push welting strip back to end of cord until fabric behind needle is tightly shirred. Continue stitching in 6" (15 cm) intervals until all welting is shirred. Insert pin through strip and cord at end to secure cord. Distribute gathers evenly. Follow page 73, steps 4 to 8.

How to Make a Shirred Box Pillow

1) Join short ends of boxing strip with ½" (1.3 cm) seam. Prepare raw edges for gathering by zigzagging over cord (page 35). Mark both edges of folds with ⅜" (1 cm) clips at quarter points.

2) Pin boxing strip to pillow front, right sides together, raw edges even, matching clips on boxing strip to pillow corners. Pull up the gathering cord to fit each side of the pillow.

3) Distribute gathers evenly, pinning as necessary. Stitch all four sides inside gathering row, stitching corners as directed on page 77, step 3.

4) Attach lower edge of the boxing strip to pillow back, except stitch only three sides, leaving one open to insert pillow form. Finish as for knife-edge pillow, page 71, steps 6 and 7a. Slipstitch opening closed.

Neckroll Pillows

Neckroll pillows are small, round bolsters with removable covers. Ribbons inserted into casings at each end allow you to draw the cover closed. Flat trims or ribbons can be sewn to the pillow for decorator accents. Fabric ruffles, gathered lace trim, or ruffled eyelet sewn into the end seams add frilly femininity. For a more tailored look, the seams are accented with welting (page 72).

✄ Cutting Directions

Cut fabric for the center tube the same length as the pillow form circumference plus 1" (2.5 cm) for seam allowances; cut the width equal to the pillow form width plus 1" (2.5 cm). Cut two end strips the same length as the pillow circumference plus 1" (2.5 cm) for seam allowances; width the same as the radius of the pillow plus 1½" (3.8 cm) for the casing and seam allowance. Cut two 3" (7.5 cm) circles to secure behind end closures.

For ruffles, cut two strips twice the desired width plus 1" (2.5 cm), with length equal to two to three times the pillow circumference. For welting, cut two bias strips equal in length to slightly more than the pillow circumference and width equal to the cording circumference plus 1" (2.5 cm).

How to Make a Neckroll Pillow

1) Pin any flat trims equal distances from ends of center tube fabric; stitch. Fold fabric in half, right sides together. Stitch ½" (1.3 cm) seam, forming tube; finish seam allowances. Press seam open. Turn tube right side out. Stitch lace or eyelet trim, ruffles, or welting to tube ends, following methods opposite.

YOU WILL NEED

Matching or contrasting fabrics for tube, two end strips, and any ruffles or cording.

Gathered lace or eyelet trim for ends, same length as pillow circumference plus 1" (2.5 cm) or flat lace or eyelet trim, twice circumference plus 1" (2.5 cm).

Flat trims or ribbons as desired, length equal to twice pillow circumference plus 2" (5 cm).

Ribbon for drawstring, ¼" (6 mm) wide and about 1½ yd. (1.4 m) long.

Neckroll pillow form.

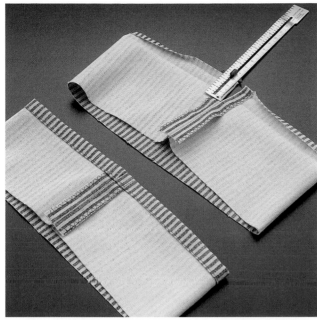

2) Press under ¼" (6 mm), then ½" (1.3 cm) on one long edge of each end strip to form casing; unfold. Stitch short ends of strip, right sides together in ½" (1.3 cm) seam, stopping 1¼" (3.2 cm) from folded end. Finish seam allowances; press open. In area of casing, stitch seam allowances flat to fabric along outer edges. Refold casing; pin. Stitch close to inner fold.

3) Pin end tube to center tube, right sides together, aligning seams and raw edges. Stitch ½" (1.3 cm) seam. Repeat for other end. Thread ribbon through casings, using safety pin or bodkin. Hand-stitch circles to centers of neckroll form ends. Insert neckroll form. Pull up ribbons and tie.

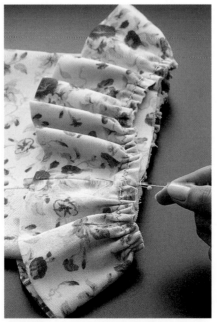

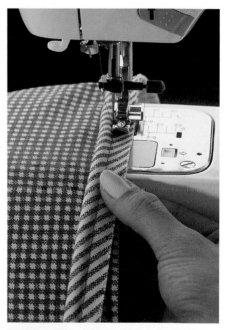

Lace or eyelet trim. Stitch short ends together in French seam. Gather flat trims by hand or machine. Pin to right side of tube ends, adjusting fullness if necessary; stitch scant ½" (1.3 cm) from edges. If applying trim and ruffles, apply trim first.

Ruffles. Prepare ruffle strips as on page 78, steps 1 and 2. Mark tube ends into fourths. Pin ruffle strips to right side of tube ends, matching marks. Pull up gathering cord to fit, distributing fullness evenly. Stitch scant ½" (1.3 cm) from edges.

Welting. Prepare and apply welting as on pages 72 and 73. If applying both welting and ruffles, apply welting first. Use zipper foot for step 3, above.

Pillow Closures

For cleaning or seasonal changes, make your pillows with closures that will allow you to remove and insert the pillow form with ease. Choose one of several closure styles, depending on the pillow style. A simple overlap closure is useful for pillow shams (page 116) as well as any decorator pillow that has a definite front side. For a reversible knife-edge or mock-box pillow, apply an invisible zipper or a conventional lapped zipper in the outer seam. Apply a centered zipper in the back of a pillow that has a corded, ruffled, or flanged outer edge.

Select conventional or invisible zippers that are about 2" (5 cm) shorter than the finished pillow. A special presser foot is required for inserting an invisible zipper. This foot unrolls the zipper coil while you stitch; after stitching, the coil and fabric roll to the inside, concealing the zipper. The presser foot is easily assembled to fit the shank, length, and needle slant of the sewing machine.

How to Sew an Overlap Closure

1) Cut pillow front as directed. Cut two pillow back pieces with same length as front and width equal to half the pillow front width plus 2¾" (7 cm).

2) Press under ¼" (6 mm), then 1" (2.5 cm) for double-fold hem on each center edge of pillow back. Edgestitch the hems in place.

3) Pin pillow back pieces to pillow front with raw edges even and hemmed edges overlapping in center. Stitch ½" (1.3 cm) seams. Turn right side out and insert pillow form or liner.

How to Sew an Invisible Zipper Closure

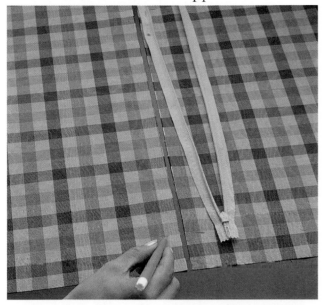

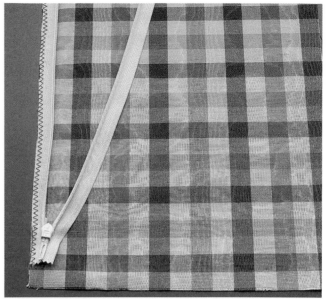

1) Steam press open zipper tape from wrong side, to unroll coils. Center zipper along one long edge of pillow back. Mark right side of pillow back at ends of zipper coil; transfer marks to front piece. Mark ½" (1.3 cm) seamlines with chalk or removable marker.

2) Open zipper; position on pillow back, right sides together, with zipper coil aligned to marked seamline and ends of zipper coil aligned to marks. Outer edge of zipper tape is near raw edge of fabric. Glue-baste or pin zipper tape in place; finish seam allowance, catching zipper tape in stitches.

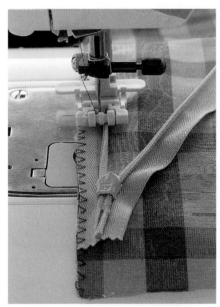

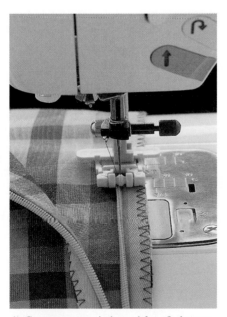

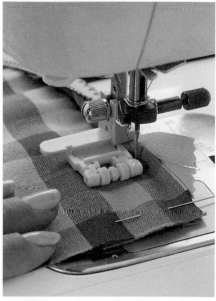

3) Attach invisible zipper foot to machine; position top of zipper coil under appropriate groove of foot. Slide zipper foot on adapter to adjust needle position so stitching will be very close to the coil; on heavier fabric, set needle position slightly away from coil. Stitch, starting at top of zipper coil, until zipper foot touches the pull tab at bottom, taking care not to stretch fabric. Secure thread at ends.

4) Secure remaining side of zipper to pillow front, as in step 2. Position coil under zipper foot; slide zipper foot on adapter to opposite side, and adjust the needle position. Bulk of fabric will be on opposite side of needle. Stitch until zipper foot touches pull tab; secure thread.

5) Close zipper; pin pillow front and back right sides together above and below zipper. Adjust zipper foot to get as close as possible to zipper. Stitch remainder of seam.

How to Insert a Centered Zipper in a Pillow Back

1) Cut pillow back 1" (2.5 cm) wider than front to allow for a ½" (1.3 cm) seam allowance at center back. Press pillow back in half lengthwise, right sides together. Center zipper along fold. Mark fold at ends of zipper coil.

2) Stitch ½" (1.3 cm) seam from pillow edge to first mark; backstitch. Machine-baste to second mark. Shorten stitch length; backstitch. Stitch to edge. Cut on fold; press seam open.

3) Center closed zipper facedown over seam, with coil on seamline and zipper stops at marks. Glue-baste or pin to seam allowances only. Finish seam allowances, catching zipper tape in stitches.

4) Spread pillow back flat, right side up. Mark top and bottom of zipper coil with pins. Center ½" (1.3 cm) transparent tape over the seam; topstitch along edges of tape. Remove tape. Tie threads on wrong side of pillow; remove basting.

Cushions

A custom cushion is made to fit a chair, bench, or window seat. It has a firm inner core of polyurethane foam wrapped with polyester upholstery batting. Knife-edge cushions are made with 1" (2.5 cm) foam. Deeper cushions are made with a boxing strip to accommodate foam with a thickness of 2" (5 cm) or more. Welting can be inserted into the cushion seams for additional design interest. Ties or hook and loop tabs may be sewn into the cushion seam to anchor it to the furniture.

✂ Cutting Directions

Make the pattern and cut the fabric, foam, and batting following steps 1 and 2, page 90 for knife-edge cushion or step 1, page 90, for box cushion. For a box cushion, cut the boxing strip with the width equal to the foam thickness plus 1" (2.5 cm) and length equal to the cushion circumference plus 1" (2.5 cm).

For the optional welting, cut 1⅝" (4 cm) bias fabric strips; piece the strips as necessary to make a length that is equal to the circumference of the cushion plus at least 1" (2.5 cm) overlap at the ends. Cut twice as much for a box cushion. Cut ties or tabs as on page 92 or 93.

YOU WILL NEED

Polyurethane foam, 1" (2.5 cm) thick for knife-edge cushion, 2" to 4" (5 to 10 cm) thick for boxed cushion.

Polyester upholstery batting.

Decorator fabric.

Paper for making pattern.

Serrated knife or electric knife, for cutting thick foam.

Cording, ⁵⁄₃₂" (3.8 mm) in diameter, for welting, optional.

How to Make a Knife-edge Cushion

1) Make a pattern of the area to be covered by the cushion, rounding any sharp corners; simplify the shape as necessary. Cut pattern; check the fit. Mark pattern for placement of ties, if desired.

2) Cut two pieces of upholstery batting, using pattern. Trace pattern on foam, using marking pen; cut ¼" (6 mm) inside marked line, using shears or electric or serrated knife. Place pattern on wrong side of fabric. Mark cutting line 1" (2.5 cm) from pattern edge; this allows ½" (1.3 cm) for seams and ½" (1.3 cm) for foam and batting thickness. Cut cushion top on marked line. Cut bottom, using top as pattern.

3) Make welting, if desired, and apply to cushion top as on pages 72 and 73. Make ties or tabs, if desired, as on page 92 or 93. Sew cushion cover as on page 71, steps 4 to 6. Place foam between batting layers. Whipstitch edges of batting together, encasing foam. Compress cushion and insert into cover; smooth cover evenly over cushion. Slipstitch opening closed.

How to Make a Boxed Cushion

1) Make pattern. Position pattern on foam; trace, using marking pen. Cut foam ¼" (6 mm) inside marked line, using electric or serrated knife. Cut two pieces of upholstery batting, adding half the foam depth around the pattern. Place pattern on wrong side of fabric. Mark cutting line ½" (1.3 cm) from edge for seam allowance. Cut cushion top on marked line. Cut bottom, using top as pattern.

2) Cover foam with batting as above, step 3. Sew cushion cover as on page 77. Compress cushion and insert into cover; smooth cover evenly over cushion. Slipstitch opening closed.

Tufted Cushion

Add button tufting to chair or bench cushions to prevent filling from shifting inside the cover. Tufting is done after the cushion is finished. Tufted cushion covers are usually not removed, so zippers or other closures are not necessary.

Use covered flat buttons with a shank. Buttons for covering are available in kits, complete with a button front and back, and tools that simplify covering the button. Dampen the button fabric just before beginning. As the fabric dries around the button, it will shrink slightly to fit smoothly.

YOU WILL NEED

Long needle, with large eye.

Strong thread such as button and carpet thread or buttonhole twist.

Flat dressmaker buttons with shanks, two for each tuft.

How to Tuft a Cushion

1) Thread a long needle with extra-strong button and carpet thread or several strands of buttonhole twist. Thread strands through button shank; tie ends to shank with double knot.

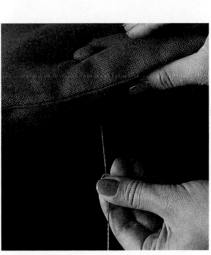

2) Push needle through cushion, pulling button tight against pillow to create a "dimple." Clip thread near needle.

3) Thread second button on one strand of thread. Tie single knot with both strands and pull until button is tight against bottom of cushion. Wrap thread two or three times around button shank. Tie double knot. Trim threads.

Cushion Ties

Attach cushions to chairs with traditional fabric ties. Ties prevent cushions from sliding and add a decorative accent to chairs.

Make ties to suit the style of the chair and cushion. Experiment with different sized fabric strips tied around the chair posts, to determine the appropriate length and width of the ties. Trim the fabric strip to desired size to use as a pattern.

✂ Cutting Directions

Cut each tie 1½" (3.8 cm) longer and 1" (2.5 cm) wider than the fabric pattern, allowing ½" (1.3 cm) for seam end and 1" (2.5 cm) for knotting the finished end. Cut two ties for each post where the ties will be attached.

How to Make Cushion Ties

1) Make two ties for each post where ties will be attached. Press under ¼" (6 mm) on long edges of each tie. Press tie in half lengthwise, wrong sides together, pressed edges even; pin.

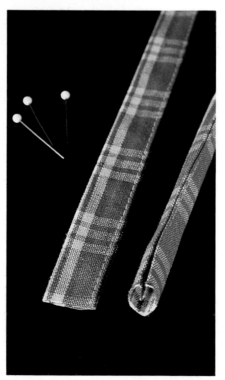

2) Edgestitch along open edge of ties. Leave both ends of tie open. Tie a single knot at one end of tie, enclosing the raw edges in the knot.

3) Pin unfinished ends of ties to right side of cushion front at marks. Pin cushion front to back, right sides together. Stitch, backstitching over ties. Finish cushion and tie to chair post.

Hook & Loop Tabs

Hook and loop tape tabs make a cushion extremely easy to attach and remove, and because they are small and inconspicuous they blend in well with furniture.

The length of the tab depends on the size of the rung or post that the tab goes around. Measure accurately because the tabs must fit snugly. Tabs may be hand-stitched to existing cushions because they do not need to be stitched in a seam.

✂ Cutting Directions

Cut tabs just long enough to go around chair post and overlap by 1" to 1½" (2.5 to 3.8 cm), plus ½" (1.3 cm) for seam; twice the finished width, plus ½" (1.3 cm).

Cut hook and loop tape 1" to 1½" (2.5 to 3.8 cm) long for each tab.

How to Make Cushion Tabs with Hook & Loop Tape

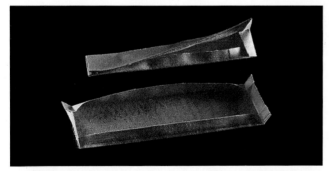

1) Make one tab for each corner. Press under ¼" (6 mm) on each edge of tab. Press tab in half lengthwise, wrong sides together. Edgestitch all four sides of tab.

2) Cut hook and loop tape for each tab. Separate hook and loop sides. Attach opposite sides of tape to opposite sides of tab. Stitch around all four sides of hook and loop tape.

3) Stitch pillow front to back. Before stuffing, pin center of tab to seam at cushion corners. Place all tabs in same direction; stitch and backstitch.

4) Finish cushion. Attach cushion to chair or bench by fastening hook and loop tabs around posts, overlapping ends to secure.

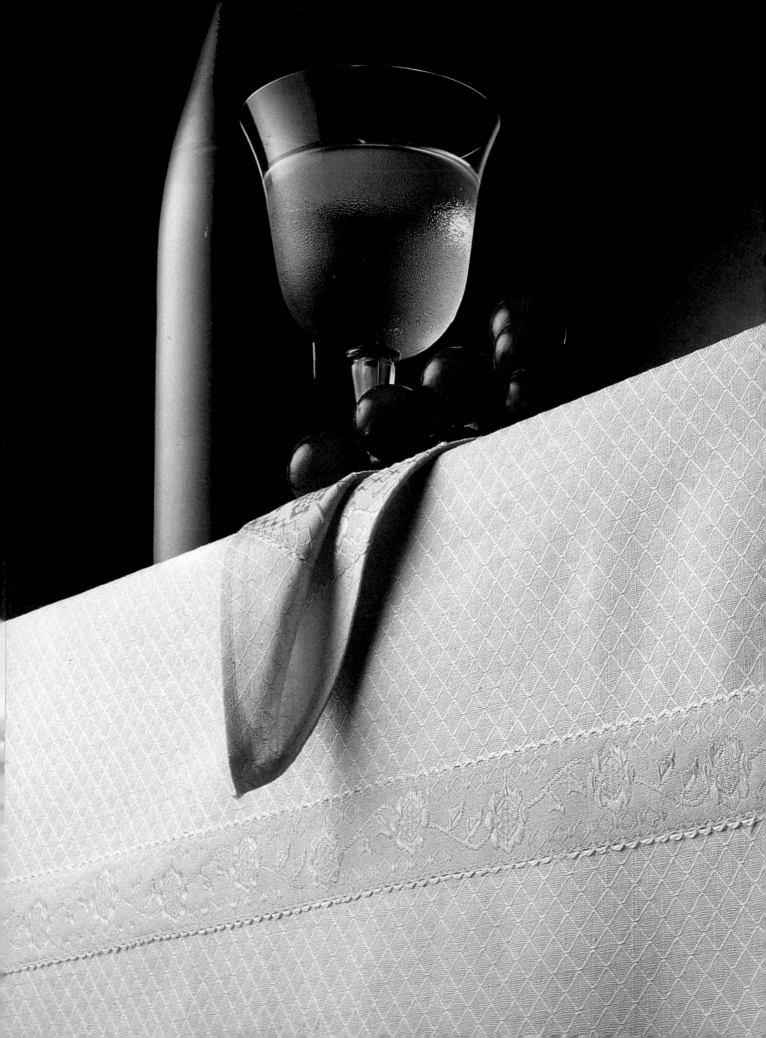

Tables

Tabletop Fashions

Customized tabletop fashions are a simple way to change the look of a room without spending too much time or money. These easy projects make good home sewing sense.

Because most tablecloths are wider than one fabric width, you must seam fabric widths together to make the tablecloth the width you need. Avoid a center seam by using a full fabric width in the center and stitching narrower side panels to it.

Do not use selvage edges in the seams as they tend to pucker. Use plain, French, or overedge seams.

Placemats, napkins, and table runners give you an opportunity to experiment with finishing techniques you may be reluctant to try on larger projects.

Selecting Fabrics

When you design tabletop fashions, look for durable, stain-resistant fabrics that have been treated to repel soil and water. Permanent press fabrics offer easy care. Drape the fabric over your arm to see how it hangs.

For everyday use, lightweight cotton is appropriate; use a lightweight tablecloth with a table pad to protect fine wood tables. For an elegant look, use a sheer lace or eyelet tablecloth over a heavier cloth.

Small random prints are easier to work with than prints that may need matching. Avoid heavily napped fabrics or fabrics with difficult-to-match design motifs such as printed plaids or stripes, diagonals, or one-way patterns.

Measuring the Table

The length of the tablecloth from the edge of the table to the bottom

Home-sewn table fashions, unlike purchased ones, are not limited to a small selection of standard sizes. When you design a tablecloth yourself, you can scale it to the exact size and shape of your table. You can also choose from an abundant supply of fabric colors, patterns, and textures that complement the decor of your room.

of the cloth is called the *drop* (right). Be sure to include the drop length in your tablecloth measurements.

Round tablecloth. Measure the diameter of the table, then determine the drop length of the cloth. The size of the tablecloth is the diameter of the table plus twice the drop length plus 1" (2.5 cm) for a narrow hem allowance. A narrow hem is the easiest way to finish the curved edge of a round tablecloth.

Square tablecloth. Measure the width of the tabletop; then determine the drop length of the cloth. Add twice the drop length plus 1" (2.5 cm) for a narrow hem allowance or 2½" (6.5 cm) for a wide hem allowance.

Rectangular tablecloth. Measure the length and width of the tabletop; then determine the drop length of the cloth. The size of the finished tablecloth is the width of the tabletop plus twice the drop length, and the length of the tabletop plus twice the drop length. Add 1" (2.5 cm) for a narrow hem or 2½" (6.5 cm) for a wide hem.

Oval tablecloth. Measure the length and width of the tabletop, then determine the drop length of the cloth. join fabric widths as necessary to make a rectangular cloth the length of the tabletop plus twice the drop length, and the width of the tabletop plus twice the drop length; add 1" (2.5 cm) to each dimension for a narrow hem allowance. Put a narrow hem in an oval tablecloth because it is the simplest way to finish the curved edge. Because oval tables vary in shape, mark the finished size with the fabric on the table. Place weights on the table to hold the fabric in place, then use a hem marker or cardboard gauge to mark the drop length evenly.

Three common drop lengths are: short, 10" to 12" (25.5 to 30.5 cm); mid-length, 16" to 24" (40.5 to 61 cm); and floor-length, 28" to 29" (71 to 73.5 cm). Short cloths end at about chair seat height and are good for everyday use. Mid-length cloths are more formal. Elegant floor-length coverings are used for buffet and decorator tables.

Round Tablecloths

To determine the yardage for a tablecloth without a flounce, divide tablecloth diameter by fabric width less 1" (2.5 cm). Count fractions as one width. This is the number of widths. Then multiply number of widths by diameter and divide by 36" (100 cm) to find the total yards (meters).

For center of flounced-edge table-cloth, subtract two times the finished depth of the flounce from the finished length of the tablecloth. Determine yardage for center as for tablecloth above.

Determine the flounce length by multiplying diameter of center by 3½; double this figure. For number of strips, divide flounce length by fabric width. Multiply number of strips by cut depth and divide by 36" (100 cm) for total yards (meters).

✂ Cutting Directions

For tablecloth without a flounce, cut center panel with length equal to tablecloth diameter plus hems. Add partial panels to form square.

For tablecloth with flounce, cut center panel with length equal to the diameter of center plus seam allowances. Add partial panels to form square. Cut strips for flounce the depth of flounce, plus hem and seam allowances and length as determined above.

How to Cut a Round Tablecloth

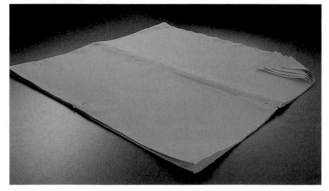

1) **Join** fabric panels, right sides together, with ½" (1.3 cm) seams to form square. Fold square into fourths. Pin layers together to prevent slipping.

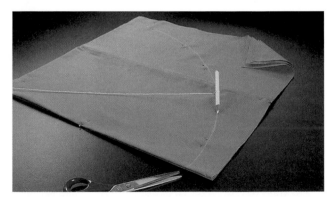

2) **Measure** a string the length of the cloth radius plus ½" (1.3 cm) for hem or seam allowance. Tie one end of string around a marking pencil; pin other end at center folded corner of cloth. Mark outer edge, using string and pencil as compass. Cut on marked line; remove pins.

How to Sew Narrow & Flounced Hems

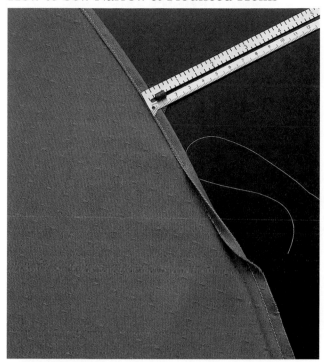

Narrow hem. Stitch around tablecloth ¼" (6 mm) from edge. Press under on stitching line. Press under ¼" (6 mm) again, easing fullness around curves. Edgestitch close to folded edge. Or use narrow hemmer.

Flounced edge. Seam strips of flounce, right sides together, to form loop. Hem lower edge. Zigzag over cord to gather raw edge (page 35). Attach flounce to tablecloth as for ruffled curtains (page 36).

How to Sew a Welted Hem

1) Multiply diameter of the tablecloth by 3½ to determine length of welting needed. Cut and join bias strips, right sides together, to cover cording (page 72).

2) Cover cording and attach to right side of cloth as for welted pillow, page 73, steps 3 to 7. Zigzag seam and press to back of tablecloth. Topstitch ¼" (6 mm) from welted seam.

Square & Rectangular Tablecloths

Make tablecloths the desired width by joining fabric widths as necessary, using full widths in the center and partial widths on the lengthwise edges. Straighten the crosswise ends of fabric (page 26) to square the corners. Use plain, French, or overedge seams.

Select the width and finish of the hem to complement the weight and texture of the fabric. Mitering is the neatest way to square corners because it covers raw edges and eliminates bulk.

Determine the amount of fabric needed for the tablecloth by dividing the total width of the tablecloth by the width of your fabric, less 1" (2.5 cm). Multiply this figure, which is the number of panels needed, by the total length of the tablecloth. Divide this number by 36" (100 cm) to get the total yards (meters) required.

Wide and Narrow Hems

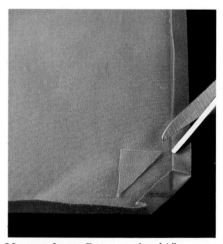

1) Wide hem. Press under ¼" to ½" (6 mm to 1.3 cm), then press under 1" or 2" (2.5 or 5 cm) hem on all sides.

2) Open out corner, leaving first fold turned under. Miter corners as for double-flange pillow, page 81, steps 3 to 7. Blindstitch or straight-stitch hem.

Narrow hem. Press under ½" (1.3 cm) on each side. Open corner; fold diagonally so pressed folds match. Press; trim corner. Fold raw edge under ¼" (6 mm). Fold again on first fold line; press. Stitch hem.

Quilted Table Covers

Quilting adds body to table coverings and provides additional protection for table surfaces. The thickness and slight puffiness of quilted table accessories also adds visual appeal. Use quilted fabrics for placemats, table runners, and table mats. Finish edges with bias binding (pages 102 and 103).

Prequilted fabrics are available, but quilting your own fabric provides the luxury of coordinating colors and prints, and the economy of making only the amount of quilted fabric needed for a project. Removable markers and a walking foot (page 14) make the channel-quilting process easy. Begin by stitching the center quilting row, and work toward the sides.

Use polyester fleece or needle-punched batting for tabletop fashions. It will retain its shape and body when laundered.

How to Machine-quilt Fabric

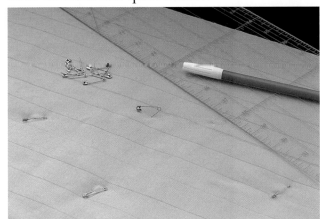

1) Cut fabric and batting to finished size, allowing for slight shrinkage resulting from quilting process. Mark channel quilting lines on right side of top fabric, using removable marking pen or chalk pencil. Test on fabric scrap for easy removal. Layer fabrics and batting; baste layers together, using needle and thread or small safety pins inserted between marked lines.

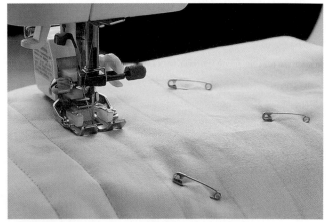

2) Attach walking foot. Stitch on marked lines, beginning with center line and working outward to each side. Stitch each line in same direction to avoid ripples. Trim outer edges as necessary before binding.

Placemats, Table Runners & Table Mats

Placemats, table runners, and table mats protect tabletops and add color and style to table settings. Use them over tablecloths, or alone to show off the beauty of wood and glass tables. The sewing techniques for placemats, table runners, and table mats are very similar.

Select fabric for mats and runners according to the general guidelines for choosing tablecloth fabrics.

Fabric may be machine quilted using the procedure described on page 101.

Finish edges of tabletop projects with wide banding (pages 104 and 105) or bias binding. To make bias binding, cut and join bias strips (page 72). Fold strip in half lengthwise, wrong sides together, and press. Open binding and press cut edges toward center. Or use a bias tape maker (page 14).

Tips for Binding Placemat Edges

Quilted fabrics. Before applying binding, stitch placemat ¼" (6 mm) from edge. Trim batting from hem area to reduce bulk in bound edge.

Slipstitched edges. Open out bias binding. Pin right side of binding to front of mat, raw edges even. Stitch on foldline. Turn binding to back of mat and slipstitch.

Topstitched edges. Open out bias binding. Pin right side of binding to back of mat, raw edges even. Stitch on foldline. Turn binding to front of mat and topstitch.

Placemats can be lined, underlined with fusible interfacing, made of quilted fabric, or sewn double for extra body. Two common finished sizes of placemats, are 18" × 12" (46 × 30.5 cm) and 16" × 14" (40.5 × 35.5 cm). Choose the best size for your table and place settings.

Table runners are usually 12" to 18" (30.5 to 46 cm) wide; make them wider if they will be used as placemats. Drop lengths vary from 8" to 12" (20.5 to 30.5 cm). Table runners may be cut on either the lengthwise or the crosswise grain of the fabric, but less piecing of fabric is required if they are cut on lengthwise grain.

Table mats protect the surface of a table without hiding the legs or base. Cut and sew a mat to the exact size of the tabletop and finish the edges.

Corners. Sandwich the fabric in binding, starting binding at center of one side. Baste binding and topstitch to corner, catching all layers. At corner, fold diagonally; baste and topstitch next side. Finish ends, right.

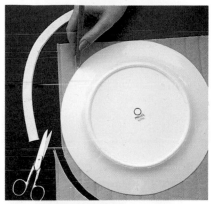

Oval mats. Shape corners of mat using a dinner plate as a guide. Before applying bias binding, shape binding to curves with a steam iron.

Finishing ends. Cut bias binding 1" (2.5 cm) beyond the end. Turn under ½" (1.3 cm); finish stitching to end of binding. Slipstitch.

Banded Placemats

Wide double banding creates a reversible placemat.

✂ Cutting Directions

Determine size of finished mat (page 103) and desired width of finished banding. Cut placemat center the size of finished mat minus two times the width of finished banding, plus ½" (1.3 cm). For each mat, cut two centers. Stitch centers, wrong sides together, a scant ¼" (6 mm) from raw edge.

Cut banding twice the finished width plus ½" (1.3 cm); length the distance around outer edge of *finished* mat plus ½" (1.3 cm). Use ¼" (6 mm) seams. Press in half lengthwise, wrong sides together. Press under ½" (6 mm) on lengthwise edges.

How to Sew Banded Placemats with Mitered Corners

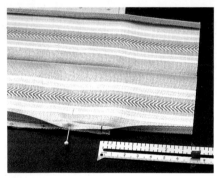

1) Mark beginning stitching point on band the width of finished band plus ¼" (6 mm). Place mark ¼" (6 mm) from corner of mat, raw edges even and right sides together.

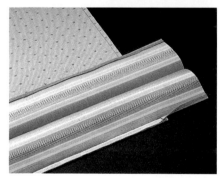

2) Mark and pin band at adjacent corner ¼" (6 mm) from edge. Pin between corners. Stitch on foldline from mark to mark; backstitch at ends to secure.

3) Fold band from mat diagonally. Mark out from corner stitching the width of finished band. Fold at mark, right sides together. Mark ¼" (6 mm) from corner of mat.

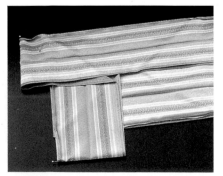

4) Repeat steps 2 and 3, above, for next two corners.

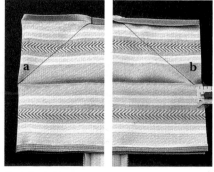

5) Mark lines for miters from previous stitching to foldline; end lines at folded edge **(a)** or ¼" (6 mm) from raw edge **(b);** stitch. Trim excess fabric. Press seams open.

6) Turn band to finished position. Fold miters on underside of band; pin folded edge of band to seamline. Slipstitch miters and edges of band.

Trimmed Placemats

Decorative ribbon trim or fabric trim finishes and accents the outer edges of these placemats. The same method may also be used to finish the outer edges of square or rectangular tablecloths (page 100).

✄ Cutting Directions

Cut the placemat 1" (2.5 cm) larger than desired finished size (page 103). Press ½" (1.3 cm) seam allowance to right side of placemat on all edges. Cut trim long enough to go around edge of placemat, plus 1" (2.5 cm). You will need approximately 61" (155 cm) for each placemat. If making your own trim from fabric, allow ¼" (6 mm) on each side for finishing. Press under ¼" (6 mm) on long sides of fabric trim.

How to Sew Placemats with Mitered Ribbon Trim

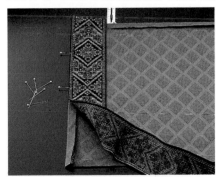

1) **Position** short end of trim ½" (1.3 cm) beyond edge of mat, aligning lengthwise edge of trim with folded outer edge of the placemat; pin.

2) **Fold** trim straight back at corner so fold is even with edge of mat. Fold trim diagonally to form right angle; press and pin. Repeat at next two corners.

3) **Fold** end diagonally at first corner to form right angle; press. Remove pins. Baste on diagonal foldlines, using pins or glue stick.

4) **Stitch** each corner of trim on diagonal foldline, stitching on wrong side and beginning at inner edge. Backstitch at beginning and end of seam to secure.

5) **Adjust** mat size or miters if necessary. Trim seam allowances of miters to ¼" (6 mm); press seams open. Press under seam allowance that extends at one corner.

6) **Baste** trim to mat, with outer edges even. Stitch outer edge, beginning at one side and pivoting at corners; backstitch. Stitch inner edge.

105

Six Ways to Make and Hem Napkins

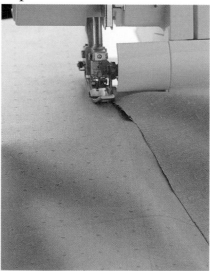

Satin stitch. Turn under ½" (1.3 cm) on all sides. Miter corners (page 100). Edgestitch along raw edge to use as guide. Use wide, closely spaced zigzag to stitch from right side over edgestitching.

Serger. Mark cutting lines of all napkins on full cloth. Serge on marked lines to cut apart and finish edges, using short, balanced overedge stitch. Serge all remaining edges.

Decorative stitch. Press under ¼" (6 mm) and stitch. From right side, stitch with a decorative stitch, using straight stitching as the guideline. Blanket stitch (shown above) gives a hemstitched look.

Napkins

Coordinating napkins are the finishing touch to your tabletop fashions. Standard finished napkins are 14" or 17" (35.5 or 43 cm) square. Before cutting the fabric, square the ends, using a carpenter's square. For fringed napkins, square the ends by pulling a yarn (page 26).

Napkin hems can be decorative. Experiment with some of the decorative stitches on your sewing machine. The hemming techniques shown here can also be used on tablecloths and placemats.

✂ Cutting Directions

Cut napkins 1" (2.5 cm) larger than finished size. One yard (meter) of 36" (91.5 cm) wide fabric yields four 17" (43 cm) napkins. A piece of fabric 45" (115 cm) square yields nine 14" (35.5 cm) napkins.

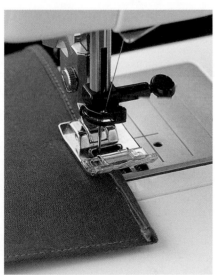

Narrow hem. Press under ¼" (6 mm) double-fold hem on opposite sides of all napkins. Edgestitch from one napkin to the next using continuous stitching. Repeat for remaining sides.

Double-fold hem. Turn under ¼" (6 mm) on all edges and press. Turn under another ¼" (6 mm). Miter corners as directed for narrow hem (page 100). Edgestitch close to folded edge.

Fringe. Cut napkins on a pulled yarn to straighten edges. Stitch ½" (1.3 cm) from raw edges with short, straight stitches or narrow, closely spaced zigzag. Pull out yarns up to the stitching line.

Bed & Bath

Bed Fashions

Custom-made bed fashions such as comforters, comforter covers, pillow shams, and dust ruffles can be ruffled or tailored to suit the decor. Chintzes, polished cottons, and sateens are good choices for most bed coverings. Sheets are another practical fabric choice; their width makes seaming unnecessary on comforters and covers.

Permanent press fabrics with soil-resistant finishes are advisable in a child's room. Select fabrics that will launder well without fading.

Comforters are a useful alternative to bedspreads. Make them reversible to change their look, and fill them with polyester batting as flat or as puffy as you wish. Decorator fabrics used for comforters should be pieced together with a full fabric width in the center of the comforter and a partial width on each side.

Comforter covers, also known as *duvet covers,* are removable for easy care. They protect new comforters, salvage worn ones, and quickly change the look of a comforter. They also eliminate the need for a top sheet and blanket on the bed.

Pillow shams are removable, decorative pillow covers. Make pillow shams plain or flanged, ruffled or trimmed, in matching or contrasting fabrics to complement the comforter and dust ruffle. Traditional pillowcases may also be trimmed with ruffles and used as pillow shams.

Dust ruffles or bed skirts are used with comforters. They may be gathered or pleated. Make them in one piece for beds that do not have a footboard. Make them in three pieces for beds that do have a footboard. Attach dust ruffles to a fitted sheet placed over the box spring or to a muslin *deck,* a piece of fabric which fits between the mattress and the box spring.

Fabrics for dust ruffles should be considered for their weight and draping quality, as well as suitability for the style of the dust ruffle or bed skirt.

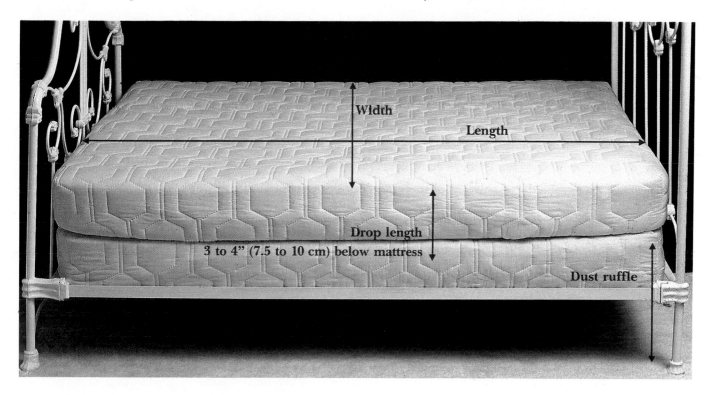

Measuring the Bed

Measure accurately to make a comforter and dust ruffle that fit the bed perfectly.

Comforters reach 3" to 4" (7.5 to 10 cm) below the mattress line. They have a *drop length* (the distance from the upper edge of the mattress to the bottom of the comforter) of 9" to 12" (23 to 30.5 cm), depending on the depth of the mattress. Determine the drop length by measuring from the top of the mattress to the top of the box spring, then adding to that figure the amount of overlap desired. Take into account fabric stiffness which may cause the comforter to stand away from the side of the bed.

To determine finished comforter size, measure from side to side across the top of the mattress for width, and from the head to the foot of the bed for length. Add the desired drop length to the length of the

bed, and twice the drop length to the width of the bed for finished measurements.

Batting for comforters is available in standard widths for beds of standard sizes; select the proper size for your comforter.

For the finished dust ruffle length, measure from the top of the box spring to the floor; for the deck, measure the width and length of the box spring.

Pillow sizes are 20" × 26" (51 × 66 cm) standard; 20" × 30" (51 × 76 cm) queen; and 20" × 40" (51 × 102 cm) king. Pillow puffiness varies, however, so make the best-fitting shams by measuring the width and length of the pillow with a tape measure across the center of the pillow. Ruffled shams made from lightweight fabrics will droop around the edges if they are cut too large.

Comforter

Comforters have the look of quilts but do not require time-consuming and intricate hand-quilting. They should reach just below the mattress line and be used with dust ruffles or bed skirts.

Comforters are made from three layers: a backing or lining, a bonded polyester batting for warmth and body, and a top layer of decorator fabric.

Because the bulk of the comforter makes machine-quilting difficult to manage, it may be hand-tufted. Tufting, or hand-tied yarn, holds the layers together and emphasizes the appealing puffiness. Place tufts 6" to 10" (15 to 25.5 cm) apart; the design of the fabric may dictate their placement.

✄ Cutting Directions

Cut and seam fabric for comforter top equal to finished size. Cut lining 8" (20.5 cm) larger than finished size for self-binding edge. Or cut lining same as top; finish edge with wide bias binding strips as for quilted placemats, pages 102 and 103.

YOU WILL NEED

Decorator fabric for comforter.

Lining for comforter.

Bonded polyester batting, proper size for bed width and cut to finished size of comforter.

Yarn, pearl cotton, or embroidery floss for tufting, washable if comforter will be laundered.

How to Sew and Tuft a Comforter

1) **Place** lining facedown on flat surface. Leaving 4" (10 cm) border, place batting on lining, then decorator fabric, right side up, edges even with batting. Hand-baste layers together with long stitches in parallel rows 8" to 10" (20.5 to 25.5 cm) apart.

2) **Fold** lining to edge of batting. Fold corners diagonally, then fold lining again over front of comforter to form 2" (5 cm) border; pin. Machine-stitch or slipstitch binding to comforter along folded edge. Slipstitch mitered corners.

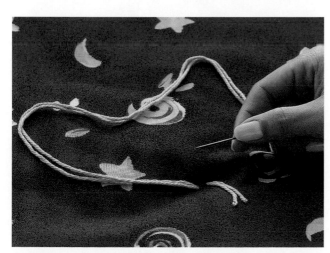

3) **Mark** positions for tufts. Thread a large needle with double strand of yarn. Working from right side of comforter, make ¼" (6 mm) stitch through all layers. Leave 1½" (3.8 cm) tail of yarn.

4) **Hold** all four strands of yarn in one hand, close to comforter. Bring needle behind four strands and over two strands to form loop; draw needle through. Pull ends to secure knot. Clip ends to ¾" (2 cm).

Comforter Cover

Change the look of a bed with a covered comforter. It can replace a top sheet and blanket, and the removable cover of the comforter makes laundering easy. Sew your own comforter, or use a purchased one of down or polyester batting.

Choose a washable, lightweight, firmly woven fabric for the cover. Sheets are good fabric choices because they do not require piecing. Seam decorator fabric together by using a full fabric width in the center of the cover, with partial widths along the sides.

Leave a 36" (91.5 cm) opening in the back of the cover for inserting the comforter. Place the opening about 16" (40.5 cm) from the lower edge on the inside of the cover so it will not show at the ends. Use snap tape, hook and loop tape, a zipper, or buttons for closure.

✂ Cutting Directions

Cut the front of the cover 1" (2.5 cm) larger than the comforter. Cut the back of the cover according to the closure method you choose. For button closures, add 5½" (14 cm) to back length. For a snap tape, hook and loop, or zipper closure, add 1½" (3.8 cm) to back length.

Cut four small fabric strips for tabs, each about 2" (5 cm) square.

YOU WILL NEED

Decorator fabric or sheets for cover and small amount of extra fabric for tabs.

Snap tape, hook and loop tape, zipper, or buttons.

Gripper snaps to hold comforter in place.

How to Sew a Comforter Cover

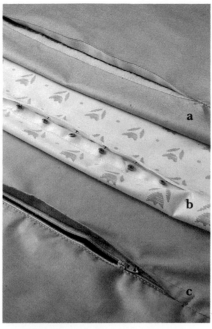

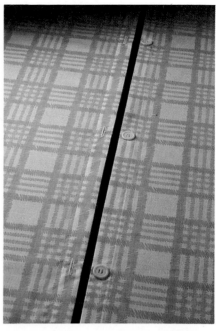

1) Press under 16" (40.5 cm) across the lower edge of the back, right sides together. If using tapes or zipper, snip the fold to mark ends of closure. Stitch ¾" (2 cm) from the fold; backstitch at snips and bastestitch across the closure area. Cut on fold; press seam open.

2a) Cut back apart on 16" (40.5 cm) fold line. Insert hook and loop tape **(a),** snap tape **(b),** or zipper **(c).**

2b) Button closure. Press under ¼" (6 mm) then 1" (2.5 cm) hem on each edge; stitch. On hem of shorter piece, make buttonholes 10" to 12" (25.5 to 30.5 cm) apart; attach buttons opposite buttonholes.

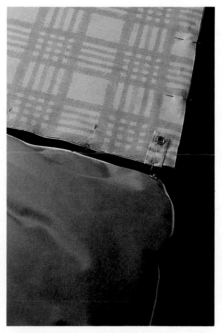

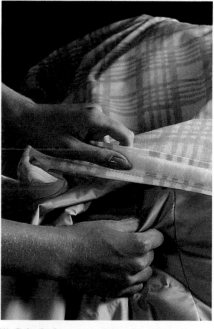

3) Pin cover front to cover back, right sides together. Trim back to fit, if necessary. For button closure, pin the shorter piece first, lapping the longer piece over it.

4) Make tabs, page 93, step 1. Attach socket side of snaps to tabs, and ball sides to corners of the comforter. Pin a tab at each corner of the cover, edges even.

5) Stitch front and back of cover together with ½" (1.3 cm) seam. Diagonally trim bulk from corners. Turn cover right side out. Insert comforter; snap cover to comforter at corners.

Pillow Shams

Pillow shams can be plain, ruffled, or trimmed with flange or banding. A sham has an overlap, or flap pocket closure, on the back to make it easy to slip a pillow into it. The easiest sham to make is cut in one piece with the ends turned under and hemmed so that the overlap is part of the fold.

To add a ruffle or coordinating flange, cut the front, back, and overlap pieces separately so that there will be a seam completely around the pillow. Seams on shams should be finished. Use French seams on one-piece shams and pillowcase shams; zigzag the seams on ruffled shams. Flange shams have enclosed seams.

✂ Cutting Directions

For one-piece sham, cut fabric same width as pillow plus 1" (2.5 cm), length equal to two times the length of pillow plus 11" (28 cm).

For ruffled sham, cut front and back 1" (2.5 cm) larger than pillow. Cut overlap 10" (25.5 cm) wide, length equal to width of pillow plus 1" (2.5 cm). Cut ruffles two times desired width plus 1" (2.5 cm), and length equal to two times the distance around pillow, plus 1" (2.5 cm).

For flanged pillow sham, cut front 5" (12.5 cm) wider and 5" (12.5 cm) longer than pillow. Cut back 5" (12.5 cm) wider and 2" (5 cm) longer than pillow. Cut overlap 5" (12.5 cm) wider than pillow and 13" (33 cm) long. This allows for ½" (1.3 cm) seams and 2" (5 cm) flange. Cut banding or trimming desired width and long enough to go around entire pillow.

For ruffled pillowcase sham, cut fabric same width as pillow plus 1" (2.5 cm); length equal to two times the length of pillow plus 1" (2.5 cm). Cut ruffle two times desired width plus 1" (2.5 cm), and length four times width of pillow. Cut facing strip 3" (7.5 cm) wide; length equal to two times the width of pillow plus 1" (2.5 cm).

How to Sew a One-piece Sham

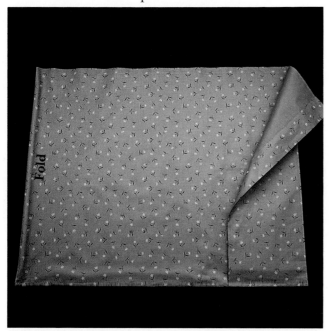

1) Stitch ½" (1.3 cm) double-fold hem at one short end. Turn under ½" (1.3 cm), then 2" (5 cm) at the other end; stitch. For overlap, press under 7½" (19.3 cm) on end with wider hem. Fold the sham crosswise, wrong sides together, so narrow hemmed edge is in pressed fold. Fold the overlap over the hemmed edge.

2) Stitch ¼" (6 mm) seam on two long sides. Trim seams to ⅛" (3 mm). Turn sham wrong side out. Press seam edges. Stitch ¼" (6 mm) from the edges for French seams. Turn the sham right side out. Insert the pillow.

How to Sew a Ruffled Sham

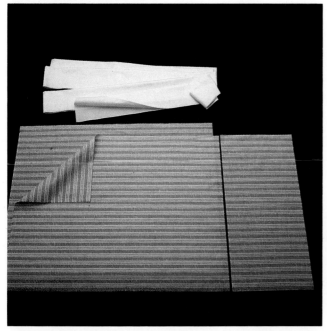

1) Stitch ½" (1.3 cm) double-fold hem on one short end of sham back. Turn under ½" (1.3 cm), then 2" (5 cm) hem on one long edge of overlap; stitch. Prepare and attach ruffle to right side of sham front, as for ruffled pillow, pages 78 and 79, steps 1 to 4.

2) Pin unfinished edge of overlap to one end of front, right sides together, with ruffle between two layers. Pin back to front, positioning back and overlap as shown. Stitch ½" (1.3 cm) seam around sham. Trim corners; finish seam allowances. Turn right side out and insert pillow.

How to Sew a Flanged Pillow Sham

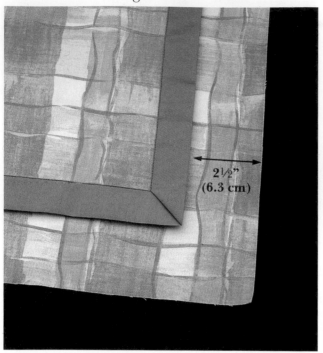

1) Position banding to front of pillow sham 2½" (6.3 cm) from edge. Miter corners, as for placemats with mitered ribbon trim, page 105. Stitch *inner* edge of band only.

2) Make sham following instructions for ruffled sham (page 117), omitting ruffle; finish seams. Turn sham right side out and topstitch along outer edge of banding. Insert pillow.

How to Sew a Ruffled Pillowcase Sham

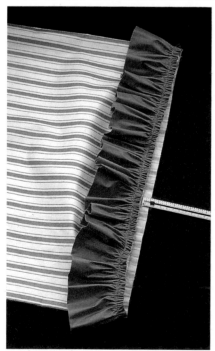

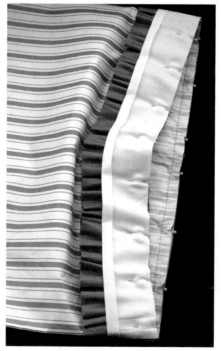

1) Fold sham, crosswise, wrong sides together; stitch French seams (page 19). Prepare and attach the ruffle to right side of open end of sham, as directed, pages 78 and 79, steps 1 to 4.

2) Press under ½" (1.3 cm) on one long side of facing strip. Join short ends of strip. Pin right side of strip to right side of pillow sham with ruffle between two fabric layers. Stitch ½" (1.3 cm) seam.

3) Press seam toward pillow sham. Edgestitch or slipstitch along pressed fold of facing strip. (Facing strip is-shown in contrasting color to make it more visible.)

Dust Ruffles & Bed Skirts

Dust ruffles and bed skirts are designed to hide the box springs and legs of a bed. They can be made to coordinate with a comforter or quilt. Gathered dust ruffles give a soft effect; pleated bed skirts are more tailored. Dust ruffles and bed skirts are gathered or pleated around only three sides of the bed.

Gathered dust ruffles can be made with either one or two layers of gathered fabric. When making a two-layered dust ruffle, gather the two layers as one piece. The type of fabric you choose determines the fullness of a gathered dust ruffle. Allow three times the fullness for lightweight fabrics; allow two to three times the fullness for mediumweight fabrics.

The directions that follow are for a gathered dust ruffle with split corners; the dust ruffle is attached to a fitted sheet. This open-cornered style, which is made in three sections, is suitable for a bed with a footboard. Dust ruffles may also be made in one continuous piece for beds without footboards.

Pleated bed skirts have deep pleats, and they are made from medium to heavyweight fabrics. The directions that follow allow for a 6" (15 cm) pleat at each end corner and the center of each side. A 1" (2.5 cm) double-fold hem is used at the lower edge and side of the skirt. The pleated bed skirt is for a bed without a footboard; the skirt is attached to a deck. The deck can be made from muslin or from broadcloth or a flat sheet in a color that matches the bed skirt.

✂ Cutting Directions

For gathered dust ruffle length, cut two pieces each the length of the box spring times the desired fullness plus 4" (10 cm) for 1" (2.5 cm) double-fold side hems; cut one piece the width of the box spring times the desired fullness plus 4" (10 cm) for 1" (2.5 cm) double-fold side hems. Dust ruffle depth is equal to distance from top of box spring to floor, plus 4" (10 cm).

For pleated bed skirt, cut deck 1" (2.5 cm) wider and 1" (2.5 cm) longer than box spring. Cut bed skirt on lengthwise grain of fabric. Cut two pieces the length of the box spring plus 18" (46 cm). Cut one piece the width of the box spring plus 18" (46 cm). Bed skirt depth equals distance from top of box spring to floor minus ¼" (6 mm) for clearance, plus 2½" (6.5 cm) for seam and hem.

YOU WILL NEED

Decorator fabric for dust ruffle or bed skirt.

Fitted sheet for deck of gathered dust ruffle.

Broadcloth, flat sheet, or muslin for deck of pleated bed skirt.

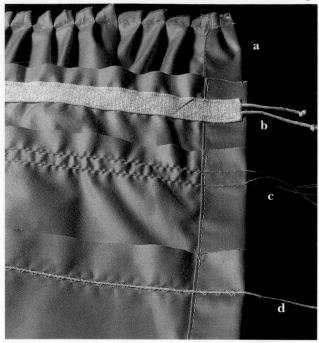

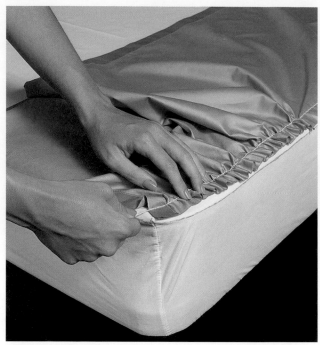

1) Stitch 1" (2.5 cm) double-fold hem along lower edges of the three dust ruffle pieces, then turn under and stitch 1" (2.5 cm) double-fold hem on both ends of each of the pieces. Gather 1" (2.5 cm) from upper edge with ruffler attachment **(a),** two-string shirring tape **(b),** two rows of bastestitching **(c),** or zigzag stitching over a cord **(d).**

2) Place fitted sheet on box spring. On sheet, mark upper edge of box spring. Mark every 12" (30.5 cm) along this line. Mark the upper edge of dust ruffle every 24" (61 cm) for double fullness, every 36" (91.5 cm) for triple fullness. Pin right sides of dust ruffle pieces along three sides of sheet, raw edges on marked line and hems overlapping at corners. Match markings on dust ruffle pieces to markings on sheet. Pull up gathering cord to fit.

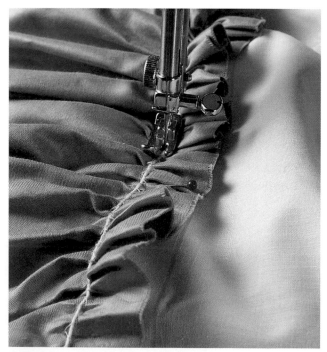

3) Remove sheet from box spring, keeping dust ruffle pinned in place. Stitch on gathering line, 1" (2.5 cm) from raw edge of dust ruffle.

4) Turn dust ruffle down over lower edge of sheet. If desired, topstitch ½" (1.3 cm) from seam, stitching through dust ruffle and sheet.

How to Sew a Pleated Bed Skirt

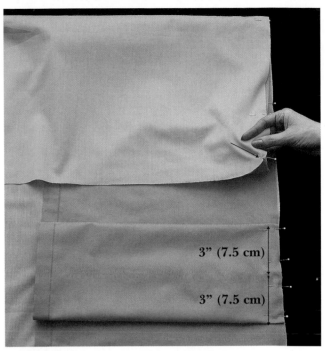

1) **Fold** deck in half lengthwise, then crosswise so corners are together. Using saucer as a guide, cut to curve corners gently. Fold curved corners in half to determine centers; mark fold with ¼" (6 mm) clips. Also, mark center of each side with clip.

2) **Stitch** skirt pieces, right sides together, on narrow ends, with short piece in center. Stitch 1" (2.5 cm) double-fold hem on lower edge of skirt and on unstitched narrow ends of skirt pieces. Pin skirt to deck, right sides together, with stitching of side hem at clip on one end of deck (arrow). Form 6" (15 cm) pleats at clip on sides and corners of deck. Seams will fall inside pleats.

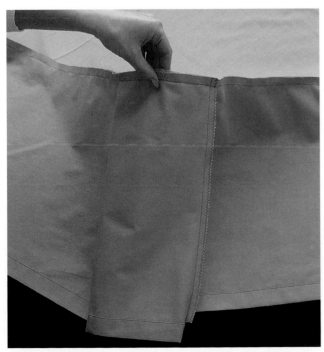

3) **Remove** skirt and machine-baste pleats. Reposition skirt on deck. Pin, right sides together. Clip center of corner pleats. Stitch ½" (1.3 cm) seam.

4) **Press** seam allowance toward deck. Press ¼" (6 mm) double-fold hem at open end of deck; stitch hem. Topstitch the skirt seam allowance to deck. Press pleats.

Shower Curtain

A shower curtain is one of the simplest curtains to sew. Valances and tiebacks can be used with the standard shower curtain. Because of its size, the shower curtain is a good place to use bold colors and prints. The instructions for sewing a shower curtain can also be used for cafe curtains or straight curtains hung with rings or hooks on decorative poles.

✄ Cutting Directions

Measure the distance from the bottom of the shower rod to the desired length. Add 10" (25.5 cm) for upper and lower hems. Measure the width of the area to be covered by the curtain and add 4" (10 cm) for side hems. Standard shower curtain liners are 72" × 72" (183 × 183 cm), so the curtain should be cut 76" (193 cm) wide if using a standard liner. Seam fabric together as needed, using French seams.

YOU WILL NEED

Decorator fabric for shower curtain.

Fusible interfacing.

Plastic shower curtain liner.

Eyelets or grommets (not necessary if buttonholes are used), equal to number of holes in plastic liner.

Shower curtain hooks, equal to number of eyelets or buttonholes.

The fabric curtain and plastic liner can hang together on the same rings or hooks, or separately on a shower rod and a spring tension rod. When they hang together, the shower curtain and the liner should be the same width.

How to Sew a Shower Curtain

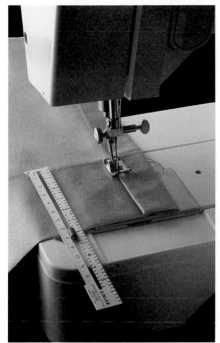

1) Turn under and stitch a 3" (7.5 cm) double-fold hem on lower edge of curtain. Turn under and stitch 1" (2.5 cm) double-fold hem on each side of the curtain.

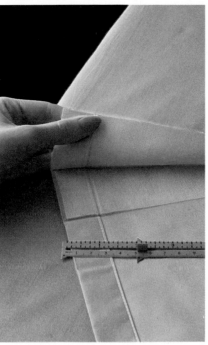

2) Press under 2" (5 cm) double-fold hem at upper edge of curtain. Open out fold and fuse a 2" (5 cm) strip of fusible interfacing along foldline. Fold again to form a double-fold hem.

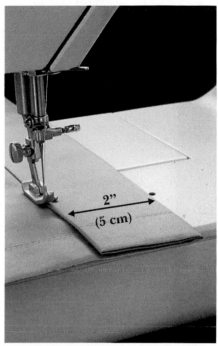

3) Edgestitch upper hem in place. Or apply fusible web, following the manufacturer's directions. Fusing adds more stability to upper edge of curtain.

4) Mark positions for eyelets, grommets, or buttonholes across upper hem, using the plastic liner as the guide for spacing holes. Position liner ¼" (6 mm) down from upper edge of curtain.

5a) Fasten eyelets securely using eyelet set and hammer or eyelet pliers. If using eyelet set, work on a piece of scrap wood or a hard surface that will not be damaged when pounding eyelets.

5b) Make vertical buttonholes, ¼" to ½" (6 mm to 1.3 cm) long. To prevent buttonholes from raveling, apply liquid fray preventer to cut edges. Insert rings or hooks.

Index

A

Accessories, sewing machine
see: Attachments, sewing machine
Adhesives, 13
All-purpose thread, 12
Attachments, sewing machine, 14
Even Feed™ foot, 14, 101
ruffler, 14, 37

B

Backstitch, machine, 18
Balloon shade, 47, 56-57
Banded placemats, 104
Bastestitching, machine, 17
Basting, hand, 20
Bath, and bed, 109-123
Batting,
needle-punched, 101
for stuffing pillows, 69
Bed skirts, 111, 119-121
Bed and bath, 109-123
Beds, 110-121
bed skirts, 111, 119-121
comforter covers, 111, 114-115
comforters, 110, 113
dust ruffles, 111, 119-120
measuring, 111
pillow shams, 111, 116-118
Bedspread,
see: Comforter

Beeswax, to strengthen thread, 20
Bent-handled shears, 13
Bias tape maker, 14
Bindings,
see: Bound edges
Blends, fabric, 9
Blindstitch,
hand, 20
machine, 27
Bolsters,
see: Neckroll pillow
Bonding fabric with fusible web, 13, 27
Borders, decorative, 102-103, 105
Bound edges,
on placemats, 102-103
on quilted fabrics, 101
on tiebacks, 42
Box pillows, 68, 74-75, 77
shirred, 68, 82-83
Box pleats, 56-57
Boxed cushion, 90
Button closure for comforter cover, 115

C

Carpenter's square, 12, 26
Casual curtains,
see: Curtains
Centered zipper, 88
Chalk, tailor's 13
Channel quilting, machine, 101
Closures,
button, 114-115
drawstring, 84-85
flap pocket, 116-117
hook and loop tape, 93, 114-115
overlap, 86, 114-115
pillow, 86-88
snap tape, 114-115
zipper, 87-88
Cloud shade, 47, 54-55
Color selection, 11
Comforter, 110, 113
Comforter cover, 111, 114-115
Compressed polyester, 69
Cording, 13, 82, 99
Corners,
gathered, 74-75
mitered, 74-75, 81, 104
pleated, 74-75
square, 74-75, 81, 104
Curtain fabric estimation chart, 25
Curtain lengths and widths,
determining, 25
Curtain rods, 29
mounting, 29
shirred pole cover, 30, 32

Curtains, 29-43
also see: Draperies, Shades
cutting fabric, 26
estimating yardage, 25
floor-length, 24-25
headings, 29-31, 44-45
hemming, 27
lining, 29, 33, 37
matching design motif, 26
measuring window, 24
rod pockets, 29-33
ruffled, 29, 34-37
shirred pole cover, 30, 32
shower, 122-123
sill-length, 24-25
tab-top, 29, 38-39
tiebacks, 29, 40-43
Cushions, 89-93
also see: Pillows
boxed, 89-90
cushion ties, 92
hook and loop tabs, 93
knife-edge, 89-90
tufted, 91
Cutting,
matching and, 26
squaring fabric ends, 26
tools, 13, 14
Cutting and matching fabric, 26
Cutting board, cardboard, 13
Cutting mat, 14

D

Deck, to fit box spring, 119, 121
Decorative edges,
on napkins, 106-107
on placemats, table runners and
table mats, 102-105
Decorative stitch, machine, 106
Decorative trims, 13
Decorator fabrics, 9
Design motif, tips for matching, 11, 26
Differential feed, on a serger, 15, 37
Double-fold hem,
curtains, 27
napkins, 107
Down, for stuffing pillows, 69
Draperies, easy pleated, 44-45
also see: Curtains
fabric estimation chart, 25
Draw draperies, 44
Drawstring pillow closure, 84-85
Drop length,
comforter, 111
table runner, 103
tablecloth, 97

Dry-cleaning fabric, 9
Dust ruffles, 111, 119-120
   also see: Bed skirts
Duvet cover,
   see: Comforter cover

E

Edge-seal system, 59-61
Edges, 15
   also see: Bound edges, Decorative
      edges, Hems
Edgestitching, machine, 17
Equipment and notions, 12-14
Estimating yardage, 25

F

Fabric adhesives, 13
Fabric selection guide, 9
Fabrics, 9-11
   blends, 9
   decorating with, 9-11
   decorator, 9
   dry-cleaning, 9
   fashion fabrics, 9
   fibers, 9
   finish, 9
   grain, 9
   insulating properties of, 9, 47, 59
   laundering, 9
   man-made fibers, 9
   marking and cutting tools, 13
   matching, 11, 26
   natural fibers, 9
   permanent finish, 9
   prewashing, 9
   repeat, 9
   selvage, 9
Fibers, fabric, 9
Fillings, pillow, 69
Finished length and width of curtains,
   24-25
Flange pillows, 68, 80-81
Flanged pillow shams, 116, 118

Flap pocket closure, 116-118
Floor-length curtains, 24-25, 27
Floor-length tablecloths, 97
Flounced hem, for tablecloth, 99
Forms and fillings,
   see: Pillow forms and fillings
Fray preventer, liquid, 13
French seam, 19
Fringed hems, 107
Fullness, estimating yardage for, 25
Fused hems, 27
Fusible interfacing, 40-43
Fusible web, 13, 27

G

Gathered dust ruffle with open
   corners, 119-120
Gathered mock box pillow, 74-75
Gathering stitch, machine, 17
Glue, 13
Grain, of fabric, 9

H

Hand stitching, 20
   also see: Hems, Machine stitching,
      Seams
   basting, 20
   blindstitch, 20
   hemming, 20
   running stitch, 20
   slipstitch, 20, 102-103
   speed-basting, 20
   tacking, 20
   tufting, 91, 113
Hand-tufting, 91, 113
Headings, 25, 29-31, 44-45
   pleated, 44-45
   with rod pocket, 29-31
Hems, 20, 27
   also see: Headings
   adding weights to, 27
   blindstitch, 20, 27
   curtain, 27

decorative stitch, 106
   double-fold, 27, 107
   edgestitched, 15
   estimating yardage, 25
   finishing, 27, 106-107
   flounced, for tablecloth, 99
   fringed, 107
   fused, 27
   napkin, 106-107
   narrow, 100, 107
   rolled hem stitch, 15
   satin stitch, 106
   side, 25, 27
   slipstitch, 20
   straight stitch, 27
   tablecloth, 97-100
   welted, 99
   wide, 100
   with mitered corners, 100
Hobbled shade, 47, 53
Hook and loop tabs, 93
Hook and loop tape, 93, 114-115
How to use this book, 7
Hybrid-mounted shade, 24, 59, 62

I

Inside-mounted shade, 24, 47, 62
Insulated lining, 47, 59-62
Insulated Roman shade, 47, 59-62
Insulating properties of fabric, 9, 47, 59
Interfacing, fusible, 40-43
Invisible zipper, 87
Iron, steam-spray, 21
Ironing board, as padded work
   surface, 21

K

Knife-edge pillows, 68, 70-76, 80-81, 90
   cushion, 90
   flange, 68, 80-81
   liner, 70-71
   mock box, 68, 74-75
   welted, 68, 72-73

L

Liner, shower curtain, 122
Lining,
  comforter, 113
  curtain, 29, 33, 37
  fabric, 9
  insulated, 59-61
  pillow, 70-71
  placemat, 103
  shades, 48-53, 56-61
Lining fabric, 9, 59
Liquid fray preventer, 13
Liquid marking pens, 13

M

Machine quilting, 101
Machine stitching, 16-19, 27
  also see: Attachments, Hand
    stitching, Hems
  backstitching, 18
  bastestitching, 17
  blindstitching, 27
  channel quilting, 101
  decorative, 106
  edgestitching, 17
  gathering stitch, 17
  needle, 17
  overedge stitch, 15
  pressure, 16
  satin stitch, 106
  speed-basting, 17
  stitch length, 17
  straight stitch, 17, 27
  tension, 16
  thread, 17
  zigzag stitch, 17
Magnetic edge-seal system, 59-61
Magnetic tape, 59-61
Man-made fibers, 9
Marking and cutting tools, 13
Marking pens, liquid, 13
Matching design motifs in fabric, 26
Material,
  see: Fabrics
Measuring,
  beds, 111
  tables, 97
  tools, 12
  windows, 24
Metal tape measure, 12
Mid-length tablecloths, 97
Mitered corners, 74-75, 81, 104
Mitered mock box pillow, 68, 74
Mitered ribbon trim, 105
Mock box pillows, 68, 74-75
Mock welted pillows, 76

Mounting,
  curtain rods, 29
  shades, 47, 59, 62
Mylar®, heat-reflecting, 59

N

Napkins, 106-107
Narrow hem, 100, 107
Natural fibers, 9
Neckroll pillow, 68, 84-85
Needle-punched batting, 101
Needle threader, 12
Needles, 12, 17
Notions, 12-14

O

On-grain and off-grain, 9
One-piece pillow sham, 116-117
Outside-mounted shade, 24, 47, 62
Oval placemats, 103
Oval tablecloth, 97
Overedge seams, 15, 18
Overedge stitch, machine, 15, 18
Overlap closure,
  for comforter cover, 114-115
  for pillow shams, 116-117
  for pillows, 86

P

Padded work surface, 21
Panel draperies, 44
Panel widths, 25
Pattern repeat, matching, 9, 25-26
Patterns,
  cushions, 89-90
  tiebacks, 40-42
Permanent finish on fabric, 9
Pillow closures, 86-88
  also see: Closures

Pillow covers,
  see: Pillow shams
Pillow forms and fillings, 69
Pillow shams, 111, 116-118
Pillowcase sham, 116, 118
Pillows, 67-93
  also see: Cushions, Pillow shams
  box, 68, 77
  closures, 86-88
  cushion ties, 92
  flange, 68, 80-81
  forms and fillings, 69
  knife-edge, 68, 70-76, 80-81, 90
  lining, 70-71
  mock box, 68, 74-75
  mock welted, 76
  neckroll, 68, 84-85
  ruffled, 68, 78-79
  shirred box, 68, 82-83
  shirred welted, 68, 82
  Turkish, 74
  welted, 68, 72-73, 76, 82
Pinch pleats, 44-45
Pins, 12
  quilting, 12
  t-pins, 12
Placemats, 102-105
  banded, 104
  binding edges, 102
  oval, 103
  quilted, 102
  square, 103
  trimmed, 105
Plain seams, 18
Plastic shower curtain liner, 122
Pleated bed skirts, 111, 119, 121
Pleated draperies, 44-45
Pleated mock box pillow, 74-75
Pleater hooks, 44-45
Pleater tape, 44-45
Pleats,
  box, 56-57
  draperies, 44-45
  pinch, 44-45
Poles,
  see: Curtain rods
Polyester batting, 69
Polyester fiberfill, 69
Polyester pillow forms, 69
Polyurethane foam, 69
Pressing, 21
Pressure, sewing machine, 16
Prewashing fabric, 9
Pulleys, on shades, 48

Q

Quilted placemats, 102
Quilted table covers, 101

Quilting, channel, 101
Quilting pins, 12
Quilts,
  see: Comforter

R

Rectangular tablecloth, 97, 100
Repeat, pattern, 9, 25-26
Ribbon, 13, 84-85, 105
Ring tape, 48
Rings, 13, 48
Rod pockets, 29-33
Rods,
  see: Curtain rods
Rolled hem stitch, on a serger, 15
Roller shade, 24, 47, 63-65
Roman shade, 47-62
  also see: Shades
  balloon, 47, 56-57
  cloud, 47, 54-55
  hobbled, 47, 53
  insulated, 47, 59-62
  lining, 47-57, 59-62
  stitched-tuck, 47, 52
Rotary cutter and mat, 14
Round tablecloth, 97, 98-99
Ruffled curtains, 29, 34-37
Ruffled pillow, 68, 78-79
Ruffled pillow sham, 116-118
Ruffled tiebacks, 43
Ruffler attachment, sewing machine,
  14, 37
Ruffles, 34-37
  also see: Headings
Ruler, wood folding, 12
Running stitch, hand, 20

S

Safety stitches, 4-thread or 5-thread, on
a serger, 16, 15, 18
Satin stitch hem finish, 106
Satin stitch, machine, 106
Seam gauge, 12
Seam ripper, 13
Seams, 15-19
  enclosed, 18-19
  estimating yardage, 25
  French, 19
  overedge, 15, 18
  plain, 18

straight, 17
  for types of fabric, 16
  zigzag, 16-17
Self-gripping fastener tape
  see: Hook and loop tape
Self-styling tape, 14
Selvage, 9
Serger, 15, 18, 106
Shades, 47-65
  also see: Curtains, Draperies
  balloon, 47, 56-57
  cloud, 47, 54-55
  estimating yardage, 25
  hobbled, 47, 53
  insulated, 47, 59-62
  lining, 47-57, 59-62
  measuring window, 24
  mounting, 47, 59, 62
  roller, 24, 47, 63-65
  Roman, 47-62
  stitched-tuck, 47, 52
Shams, pillow, 111, 116-118
Shaped tiebacks, 40-42
Shears, 13
Shirred box pillow, 68, 82-83
Shirred pole covers, 30, 32
Shirred welted pillow, 68, 82
Shirred welting, 82
Short tablecloth, 97
Shower curtain, 122-123
Side hems, 25, 27
Sill-length curtains, 24-25
Slipstitch, hand, 20, 102-103
Snap tape, 114-115
Speed-basting,
  hand, 20
  machine, 17
Square corners, 74-75, 81, 104
Square placemat, 103
Square tablecloth, 97, 100
Squaring fabric ends, 26
Stitch length, sewing machine, 16-17
Stitched-tuck shade, 47, 52
Stitches,
  backstitch, 18
  bastestitch, 17, 20
  blindstitch, 20, 27
  channel quilting, 101
  decorative, 106
  edgestitch, 17
  gathering, 17
  hand, 20
  hem finishes, 27, 106-107
  length, 17
  machine, 15-19, 27
  overedge, 15
  running, 20
  safety, 15, 18
  satin, 106
  serger, 15, 18, 106
  slipstitch, 20, 102-103
  straight, 17, 27
  zigzag, 17
Straight seams, 15, 17
Straight stitch plate, sewing machine, 17
Straight stitches, 16-17, 27
  bastestitch, 17, 20
  edgestitch, 17

gathering stitch, 17
running stitch, 20
slipstitch, 20, 102-103
Straight tiebacks, 40-41, 43
Straightening crosswise ends of fabric, 26
Synthetic fabrics, 9

T

T-pins, 12
Tab-top curtains, 29, 38-39
Table covers, quilted, 101
Table mats, 102-103
Table runners, 102-103
Tablecloths, 96-100
  drop lengths, 97
  hems, 97-100
  measuring the table, 97
  oval, 97
  rectangular, 97, 100
  round, 97, 98-99
  square, 97, 100
Tables, 95-107
  also see: Napkins, Placemats,
    Tablecloths, Table covers, Table
    mats, Table runners
Tabs, cushion, 93
Tacking, hand, 20
Tailor's chalk, 13
Tape measure, spring-return, 12
Tapes,
  magnetic, 59-61
  pleater, 44-45
  ring, 48
  self-styling, 14
  twill, 53
Tension, sewing machine, 16
Thimble, 12
Thread, 12, 17
Tiebacks, 29, 40-43
  bound, 42
  ruffled, 43
  shaped, 40-42
  straight, 40-41, 43
Ties, cushion, 92
Timesaving notions and equipment,
  14-15
Tools,
  cutting, 14
  marking, 13
  measuring, 12
Trimmed pillow sham, 111, 116-118
Trimmed placemats, 105
Trimmers, 13
Trims, decorative, 13
Tufted comforters, 113
Tufted cushion, 91
Turkish pillows, 74
Twill tape, 53

U

Upholstery batting, polyester, 69

V

Valances, 24

W

Walking foot, sewing machine, 14, 101
Weights, 27
Welted hem for tablecloth, 99
Welted pillows, 68, 72-73, 76, 82
Wide hem, 100
Widths, finished, determining for curtains, 25
Window measurement, 24
Windows, 23-65
  also see: Curtain rods, Curtains, Draperies, Shades, Tiebacks
  measuring, 24
Work surface, padded, 21

Y

Yardage, estimating, 25
Yardstick, 12

Z

Zigzag seams, 19
Zigzag stitch, machine, 16-17
  gathering stitch, 17
Zippers,
  centered, 88
  invisible, 87